MAKING PEACE
WITH YOUR
MOM

H. Norman Wright
& Sheryl Wright Macauley

BETHANY HOUSE PUBLISHERS
Minneapolis, Minnesota

Making Peace With Your Mom
Copyright © 2007
H. Norman Wright and Sheryl Wright Macauley

Cover design by studiogearbox.com
Cover photo by Charles Maraia/Getty

Unless otherwise identified, Scripture quotations are from the HOLY BIBLE, NEW INTERNATIONAL VERSION®. Copyright © 1973, 1978, 1984 by International Bible Society. Used by permission of Zondervan Publishing House. All rights reserved.
Scripture quotations identified AMP are from the Amplified Bible. Old Testament copyright © 1965, 1987 by the Zondervan Corporation. The Amplified New Testament copyright © 1958, 1987 by the Lockman Foundation. Used by permission.
Scripture quotations identified NASB are taken from the NEW AMERICAN STANDARD BIBLE®, © Copyright The Lockman Foundation 1960, 1962, 1963, 1968, 1971, 1972, 1973, 1975, 1977. Used by permission.

All rights reserved. No part of this publication may be reproduced, stored in a retrieval system, or transmitted in any form or by any means—electronic, mechanical, photocopying, recording, or otherwise—without the prior written permission of the publisher. The only exception is brief quotations in printed reviews.

Published by Bethany House Publishers
11400 Hampshire Avenue South
Bloomington, Minnesota 55438

Bethany House Publishers is a division of
Baker Publishing Group, Grand Rapids, Michigan.

Printed in the United States of America

Library of Congress Cataloging-in-Publication Data

Wright, H. Norman.
    Making peace with your mom : 8 steps to a healthier mother-daughter relationship / H. Norman Wright and Sheryl Wright Macauley.
        p.   cm.
    Summary: "Addresses the relationship between mothers and daughters within a Christian context and how it can influence the health of a daughter's other relationships later in life. Topics include mothering styles, setting boundaries, and breaking free from guilt and perfectionism"— Provided by publisher.
        ISBN-13:   978-0-7642-0290-2 (pbk.)
        ISBN-10:   0-7642-0290-1 (pbk.)
        1. Daughters—Religious life. 2. Mothers and daughters—Religious aspects—Christianity. I. Macauley, Sheryl Wright. II. Title.
    BV4551.3.W75   2006
        248.8'43—dc22   2006026445

In keeping with biblical principles of creation stewardship, Baker Publishing Group advocates the responsible use of our natural resources. As a member of the Green Press Initiative, our company uses recycled paper when possible. The text paper of this book is comprised of 30% post-consumer waste.

H. NORMAN WRIGHT is a licensed marriage, family, and child therapist, as well as a certified trauma specialist. A graduate of Westmount College, Fuller Theological Seminary, and Pepperdine University, Dr. Wright has received two honorary doctorates from Western Conservative Baptist Seminary and Biola University. He has taught at the graduate level at both Biola University and Talbot Seminary. At the present time he is research professor of Christian education at Talbot School of Theology.

The author of more than seventy books, Dr. Wright has pioneered premarital counseling programs throughout the country, and he conducts seminars on many subjects, including marriage enrichment, parenting, and grief recovery. His current focus is in crisis and trauma counseling and critical incident debriefings within the wider community.

Norm and his wife, Joyce, live in Bakersfield, California. His hobbies include bass fishing, gardening, and training his golden retriever, Shadow, as a therapy response dog.

SHERYL WRIGHT MACAULEY is an international award-winning nail artist and instructor specializing in creating miniature paintings on fingernails. She has designed and created fingernails for the New York Fashion Show. She previously teamed with her dad, H. Norman Wright, as the illustrator for *The Perfect Catch* and *That's a Keeper*. This is the first book they have written together. Sheryl and her family live in Bakersfield, California.

CONTENTS

INTRODUCTION

This book is a team effort in more ways than one. First, it reflects the experiences and insights my dad, Norm Wright, and I have had both personally and professionally. In his forty-plus years of counseling, Dad has seen the painful effects of difficult family situations and broken relationships. Thankfully, he and I have also been blessed to see how God, our heavenly Father, has brought hope and healing to many families—including our own. Because of my rebellion while growing up, as well as other circumstances (which you'll read about), my relationship with my mom and dad wasn't always the best, particularly in my twenties. I wish our struggles hadn't occurred, but I can say they have given me a fuller perspective on the wide range of mother-daughter relationships. Interestingly, my work as a manicurist has also played a part in this book. Dad says that I have helped as many women as some counselors have while I worked on their nails. I guess that could be true, because it does seem that many women who would never talk to a counselor or pastor share their experiences with me and are looking for insights.

The second way this book is a team effort is that it is based on an exclusive national survey of women. Grown daughters were invited to share their own stories about their relationships with their moms. We think there's much to be gained from the thoughts and experiences of others.

For me, I was the firstborn and very much my dad's shadow when I was young. This is not unusual, because after the age of four most little girls switch from wanting to be with their mother to adoring their father—even standing by the front door when it's time for Dad to come home.

My father and I are extremely outgoing and very similar in personality. From early on, he encouraged me to experience outdoor activities and athletics. When I was seven, my brother, Matthew, was born. Soon my parents realized that his development wasn't normal. Doctors and numerous tests confirmed that he was severely mentally retarded.

As much as a retarded child is a gift to a family, Matthew needed a tremendous amount of extra care and work. It's amazing, though, how the Lord uses unusual family dynamics to provide the opportunity to balance situations that could otherwise tear families apart. Mom was an amazing caregiver to both of us, but as to be expected, she had to spend much more time caring for Matthew than for me. Even so, I didn't really notice because I was much older and in every sense a daddy's girl. I adored my mother but shared more with my father.

In my teens I became more independent. My relationship with Mom was good, with only a few bumps during my high school years—which is not unusual for teenage girls. I was involved with our high school church group and I had opportunities to go to retreats and weekend camps.

I don't think my parents were aware at the time that there was quite a bit going on in my mind. I was very artistic but not sure how to channel that talent. I wanted to fit in with my friends, but artsy kids were considered weird, so I stuffed it. After taking a few art classes, though, my parents began to realize that I really was quite artistic.

After high school, I attended Biola College. I have to say it was rather intimidating attending the same school where my father was a professor. In the dorms, my roomie and I hit it off, but not in the most positive ways. Our activities included sneaking out, smoking, and a few other things I don't want to mention.

After a year at Biola, I entered my twenties and began to drift down the wrong path. I became a little distant from both of my parents. If I did need to share something personal, I would go to my mom because I didn't want to see the disappointment on my father's face when he learned about my activities.

I was twenty-eight when I got married, and shortly after, a shift began. Mom and I began to share more with each other and I learned much about her history, thought processes, and the hidden rebel in her—and I mean hidden. She shared extensively about her childhood and teen years. No doubt I had heard some of it before, but I probably wasn't paying attention. It was fascinating to learn more about her and realize how much I really was like her.

For years, my husband, Bill, and I tried in vain to have children. Through prayer and encouragement from trusted family and friends, we decided to adopt. How the Lord sent a birth mom to us can only be described as a miracle. A young Christian girl who loved the Lord and was at the end of her pregnancy was searching for adoptive parents. We met, and from start to finish it was a mere six weeks. On the day Shaelyn was born, amongst the tears and joy, there was a sudden surge in my soul of *Help, I need my mommy!* There was a shift in the universe, and suddenly I began to understand my mother more than ever.

At some point, most women in their thirties and forties look into the mirror and realize, "Oh my goodness, I've turned into my mother!" For me this was a relief. I realize how much I've learned from my mother—especially in spiritual matters—and I want my daughter to experience what a precious soul my mother has. If I can be half the godly mother and wife she is, I will be happy. Of course, cute idiosyncrasies come along with it, but I won't mention those!

As an older parent (we were forty when Shaelyn was born), I feel blessed that my daughter could get to know her grandparents, especially my mother. I can't remember when she wasn't there for me emotionally and spiritually. She was such a great role model during my rebellious years, even though I didn't appreciate it then. It actually annoyed me how well-grounded she was. There's a depth to her that brings stability in the midst of difficulty and pain. She has shaped my life in more ways than I realized even ten years ago. Mom is one of the most nonjudgmental women I know.

I believe this gift was acquired from her mother, who was precious and sweet and spiritually strong. During the past twenty years I have realized I can go to Mom with any problem. Even if she was disappointed in me, she did not judge or condemn me for my actions. She would encourage me to go to Jesus and ask for direction and help. I've always respected her, but that respect increases almost daily, and coauthoring this book has helped me realize how close we have become since I became a mom.

Looking back at my childhood, I had no idea that in some ways I grew up in a dysfunctional home. The word *dysfunctional* is viewed by many as a negative word. The dictionary defines dysfunctional as: (1) not operating normally or properly; and (2) unable to deal adequately with normal social relations. I view dysfunctionality in our family as "not operating normally"—at least how the world views a "normal" family.

Matthew and our lives surrounding his care was a gift. He taught me so much in patience and compassion. So many of the situations I experienced through my "colorful" life I could not have handled without the lessons I learned in our "dysfunctional" family, or by watching my mother care for Matthew and our family with such honesty and grace. In fact, it's amazing how she efficiently and unselfishly juggled the demands on her. And it's strange that she now compliments me on how I juggle my priorities and wishes she could be more like me! She *is* like me—only more proficient.

Imagine being married to a counselor, professor, and writer, handling a severely retarded child and an independent, strong-willed daughter, and still keeping a spotless house. I would call that juggling pretty well. I truly can't say that her interaction with me was missing in any way.

I happen to be a blend of my mother's and father's personalities. I had to take two opposite personalities and try to learn how to balance them. My parents are textbook examples of "opposites attract." Mother is a classic introvert and my father is an extrovert like me. They have a strong marriage despite the challenges they've faced over the years. Besides acquiring my mother's compassion and forgiving nature, I also have my father's outgoing, strong, opinionated side. I believe having her characteristics and watching how she lives has helped balance me. However, I do have the tendency to forgive too much and allow myself to be too vulnerable, so I end up being hurt by people who take advantage of me. Thank goodness for my dad's side!

But then I tend to swing completely to the opposite side. I am a true artist with a recovering alcoholic nature who lives a life of extremes. Whether my mom realizes it or not, she has been the catalyst for calming my wild side.

The only reason our relationship might have been lacking was because of my choice of lifestyle in my early twenties. We were not that close because I was living a life that neither of my parents approved of. I sought balance in alcohol, drugs, and friends. I was the one who caused the distance, not my mother. Only because of my parents' constant prayers and always being there when I needed them was I able to work my way back to the faith that Mom and Dad had instilled in me at an early age. Only then did our mother-daughter relationship really begin to blossom!

After Shaelyn's birth, my parents moved within three miles of us to be close to their only grandchild. My daily conversations with Mom are one of the few positive constants in this crazy world we live in. I wake in the morning looking forward to hearing her voice, and I look forward to speaking with her at night about the events of the day. Spending time with my daughter and "Grammy," as three generations, has also become among the most cherished moments of my life.

Lately, I've been having some health problems. My fire fighter husband is at the fire station a few nights each week. If I'm having a hard day, Mom will come over and spend the night just to be with Shaelyn and me or to help in any way.

What I appreciate most those nights are the memories she is making with Shaelyn. Interacting with loving grandparents is so important. Many people my age do not have their parents around anymore. Until August 10, 2006, Shaelyn also had her other grandmother, and even though she lived seven hours away, we saw her at least a few times a year and spoke on the phone regularly.

I remember the impact my grandmothers had on my life, and for Shaelyn to have such involved grandmothers is priceless. I can't think of anything I *don't* appreciate about my mother's involvement.

As I hinted before, my mother was greatly influenced by her mother (my Nana), who was born in the San Francisco area in the early 1900s. She also had a very godly mother who loved the Lord with all her soul. She was the kind of woman you just wanted to be near. When I was young, I just wanted to sit with her. We didn't have to talk; just being in the same room was what I imagined it would be like in the presence of the Lord.

She had a way about her I can't really explain. Like my mom, she was very nonjudgmental—a woman of poise, grace, and prayer. Being very close, Nana and Mom shared spiritual conversations and prayed together until my grandmother died at the age of ninety-five. Even toward the end of Nana's life, despite moments of dementia, she never lost her knowledge and faith in the Lord.

My mother is very much like Nana—strong, yet gentle with a deep relationship with the Lord that she will share with anyone. Growing up and watching this sweet yet strong example of a godly woman, much like many women in the Bible, had a great impact on my life. As I said earlier, besides having so many people praying for me through my wild years, I believe my mother was truly the one responsible for my recovery.

Her unconditional love makes me think, "This must be how God feels about me." No matter how many times I wander off the path, both the Lord and my mother are waiting for me with open arms.

My dad and I pray that through this book, you too will realize how much God loves you and wants to see you healed and at peace with your mom. We hope the stories and experiences from the many women who have contributed to this resource will help you move forward and give you a sense of hope.

Chapter One

TELL ME ABOUT YOUR MOTHER

—☕—

"Tell me about your mother."

Doris gave me a puzzled expression when I made the request. She was a middle-aged career woman holding a management-level position. "What does my mother have to do with why I'm here?" she replied. "I came for counseling because of the difficulties I'm having at work. My mother lives three thousand miles away."

"Tell me about your mother."

Lorianne glanced at the floor defensively, then looked up at me. Tears were welling up in her eyes. "I don't like talking about her," she began softly. "I hear her in my head most of the time. Is there some connection between her and my reasons for seeing you?" Lorianne had come for counseling because of her outbursts with her family, which intensified twice a year just before her mother came to visit.

"Tell me about your mother."

Denise's eyes brightened with my invitation to speak. "Mom was great. She taught me to be independent and to believe in myself. Oh, she still has an opinion, but she tells us to take her advice or leave it. Either way is all right with her," she said, smiling. "All of us enjoyed our relationship with her as we were growing up. Perhaps that's why I feel good about myself as a woman today. She gave me a good sense of security in who I am, not just in what I do."

"Tell me about *your* mother."

How would you, an adult daughter, respond to that statement? I'm sure many thoughts and feelings about your mom rise to the surface. Some may be pleasant and some unpleasant. Later in this chapter you'll have an opportunity to put them in writing.

A LIFE-SHAPING RELATIONSHIP

Our lives are built on relationships; they are among the most significant elements of life. We were created to be connected to others. People around us shape who we are, what we believe, and who and what we become. This is especially true of the mother-daughter relationship. It affects all areas of your life, as Henry Cloud and John Townsend explain:

Not only do we learn our patterns of intimacy, relating and separateness from Mother, but we also learn about how to handle failure, troublesome emotions, expectations and ideals, grief and loss, and many of the other components that make up our "emotional IQ"—that part of us that guarantees whether or not we will be successful at love and work. In short, the following two realities largely determine our emotional development:

1. How we were mothered.
2. How we have responded to that mothering.[1]

These two issues really do determine who you are as a person today.

If your mothering was negative, you may have developed a pattern of mistrusting, which can continue the rest of your life if not confronted. Some daughters become combative and aggressive. In order to avoid being controlled, they try to control others. Many respond to mothering, in any form, in a defensive or reactive way.

When there are unresolved issues with Mom, two important factors are at work. One has to do with your feelings for your mother, the hurts you experienced, and the needs she didn't meet. Have you identified these feelings, hurts, unmet needs? The second factor is the dynamics and patterns of relating, which you learned as you interacted with your mom. As you consider these issues, realize that the first one concerns how you feel today about your past and the other deals with how you may be repeating the patterns from your past.[2]

Your future is tied to your past. Your early relationship with your mother is the foundation upon which you will build all of your future relationships. You either received approval and affirmation—and internalized those positive feelings—or you received messages of disappointment, which turned into the way you view yourself. So the portrait you've painted of yourself was not as much by your hand but the hand of your mother.

YOUR FUTURE IS TIED TO YOUR PAST

An unhealthy, destructive, or painful mother-daughter relationship can warp future adulthood relationships if you don't come to grips with what happened and its effect. For example, some women connect with others who have many of their mother's most destructive characteristics. Perhaps it's because they are comfortable with these characteristics since they know them so well. Or it could be the woman thinks that if she can change a person or win his or her acceptance, it will prove that when she was growing up, the defect wasn't in her after all. Do you identify with these thoughts in any way?

Some daughters are so protective because of what occurred in the past that they reject or hurt others who remind them of their mother. They're on the defensive most of the time and give people little opportunity to connect.

Some women actually choose to marry a man who was like their mother. But what is especially unfortunate is the grown daughter who attempts to create in her own children the loving mother she never had. Of course this has a detrimental effect upon the children, so she repeats what her mother did in some way. When we see patterns like this, we see a woman who is still connected to her mother and hasn't yet learned to separate in a healthy way.[3] The good news is that it *is* possible to make sense of a difficult relationship and enjoy healing.

M-O-T-H-E-R

When the word *mother* is mentioned, what image comes to mind? Close your eyes and let your memories create your thoughts and feelings. What kind of an emotional response do you experience? If someone says, "I see more of your mother in you every day," is that a compliment or an insult?

Many women do enjoy a close and pleasant relationship with their moms. Over the years, I have asked variations of the following question: "What do you feel are your mother's positive qualities?" Here are some responses I have received:

- "Mom has always been there for me."
- "She met my emotional needs."
- "She gave me my creativity."
- "Mom was affectionate, affirming, and firm."
- "She taught me all the basics of life and handling a home."
- "She protected me from my dad."
- "She stood by my side when my daughter was so ill."
- "She taught me to be self-reliant. I had a good model."
- "She raised me to love God and see how much God loves me."
- "She always had a sensible answer for me."

Of course, to others the word *mother* creates stained visions— Mom as a martyr or critic or punisher or invader. Here are some of the statements I have received over the years in response to the question, "What do you feel are the negative qualities of your mother?"

- "She was never there for me as a child."
- "She abandoned me as a child."

- "She's too critical of whatever I do."
- "She put me in the middle of her arguments with Dad, and I still carry those emotional scars."
- "Our relationship is usually strained. She never calls me."
- "She's the denial queen."
- "She allowed other family members to abuse me."
- "No encouragement growing up."
- "She turned me off to marriage."

"What I fear the most is repeating the past," I've heard some say. "I don't want my mother's life. I don't want to become her, but I see it happening all over again. I hear her voice when I shop, when I eat, when I clean the house. I have a choice. Listen to the voice and do what it says and become like her, or don't conform and rebel—either way it's letting her control my life. I'm not sure what to do. . . ."

One writer describes the impact and influence of a mother in this way:

> She is slower than a speeding bullet, unable to leap tall buildings in a single bound. Yet she has the power to wound you with words and to stop you in your tracks with a disapproving glance. A recent frustrating exchange with her may have dampened your mood for days on end, and conflicts the two of you had long ago may still echo inside your head. She is your mother and, as such, the one person on earth most likely to relegate you—yes, you, a grown-up, competent, capable woman, perhaps a working woman, a corporate executive or respected professional, perhaps a busy student off on your own for the first time; perhaps a wife and mother yourself; perhaps a woman whose own children are grown—to the temporary status of raving lunatic.[4]

The idea of Mom having superhero powers may be related to our high expectations for mothers. Motherhood has been seen as a sacred and exclusive child-rearing role. Still, the view that mothers were expected to make children the focus of their lives didn't take root until the early nineteenth century. By the twentieth century, our society had defined motherhood as a mandate from heaven, although it insisted on the right to define it to the culture's own terms. In 1905, in a speech before the National Congress of Mothers, President Theodore Roosevelt said, "As for the mother, her very name stands for loving unselfishness and self-abnegation, and in any society fit to exist it is fraught with associations which renders it holy."

A mother's duty was defined for her. *She* (not the father) was responsible to raise their children into law-abiding, God-fearing citizens for the good of the family and our country. She received messages that *her* guidance and vigilance was vital, and that one slip could scar a child forever. *She* was the parent who was held most accountable for how her children turned out.

Heaven does indeed have a mandate for motherhood; but heaven's Ruler has the right to define what that means, even if it is contrary to society's definition. Our culture has offered several inadequate responses to the mandate for mothering. By identifying them, mothers can raise motherhood to a healthier level of functioning— and in the process, bequeath to their daughters healthier ways of living and relating to others.

Society says that a sign of a good mother is a good daughter. If you don't measure up, who does this reflect upon? Mom. If you mess up, people will think she messed up. Perhaps this is why so many rules were established for you when you were young. And who enforced those rules? For most daughters, Mom was the enforcer.

Dr. Paula Caplan, the author of *Don't Blame Mother*, describes the dilemma many daughters experience:

"We are so vulnerable to what our mother thinks of us. When she seems to have reservations about us, we are devastated, whether we are children, teenagers, young adults, or middle-aged or old women. Our mother's power to make us feel inadequate often makes us angry—we may even hate her for it." When you're young you can't run away to get affirmation from others, and as an adult most don't want to run away and sever their relationship with Mother. Dr. Caplan continues, "What most of us want is not to banish our mother from our lives, but to end both the power to make us feel bad and our guilt over our power to make them feel like failures."[5]

YOUR MOTHER'S INFLUENCE

Making Peace With Your Mom is the second book I've written recently about grown daughters and their parents. Like *A Dad-Shaped Hole in My Heart,* I wanted this book to be more than a source of information and help. I wanted it to be an opportunity for daughters to tell their stories. Many had never shared their experiences in an in-depth manner before. For some, the pain of their losses hasn't subsided. For others, it was more of a positive reflection, since they were fortunate enough to have had a mother who responded as a mother should.

Women across the country were asked to complete a survey of nine questions in order to gain insights into the very important relationship between a daughter and her mother. Before listening to their responses, though, we'd like you to take time to evaluate your past and present relationship with your mom by answering the same questions. Hopefully this will help you understand yourself—and your mother—in a new way.

1. How would you describe your relationship with your mother?

_____

_____

2. In what way was your mother there for you?

_____

_____

3. In what way wasn't your mother there for you?

_____

_____

4. Describe how your mother has influenced or shaped your life (either negatively or positively).

_____

_____

5. If your relationship was lacking, what have you done to overcome this?

_____

_____

6. What do you appreciate the most *and* the least in your mother's involvement with you?

_____

_____

7. If your mother's interaction was missing in your life, how did you fill this void?

_____

_____

8. What are three rules your mother taught you about life?

_____

_____

_____

9. At this point in your life, what would you like to be able to say to your mother?

_____

_____

As you listen to the experiences of other women throughout this book, be aware that they could generate various responses from you, including:

"That's *my* story."
"It's so negative."
"I'm glad that wasn't me."
"That makes me angry."
"I wish I could have experienced that."
"I'm more thankful now for my relationship with Mom after reading that."
"What would I do in that situation?"

Making peace with your mom involves a journey. But as these stories attest, you are not alone. Victories are gained one step at a time. So let's continue by hearing how women describe their relationships with their moms.

Since about the age of twelve or thirteen (I'm now thirty-one), my relationship with my mother has been rocky and distant. My mom left when I was almost thirteen years old, and I spent the first few years after she left wanting nothing or very little to do with her. Our relationship has been extremely painful, with many fights and arguments along the way. There have been a lot of tears and lots of anger, resentment, bitterness, and unforgiveness on my part. We have struggled so much at times, I wondered if we would ever make it. It has not been until the last few years that she and I have come into a new and different space, where we—mostly me—have been able to let go of some of the past and simply be in the present. We are learning to do this all the time. My mom and I are currently experiencing the best relationship we have known in a very long time. In fact, I recently said to my mom that I am at the most peace with her that I have ever been, and I am truly thankful for this!

Difficult. I have always felt like I disappointed her by not being as beautiful as she was when she was young. The quality of my character seems to be immaterial to her. She doesn't seem interested in my scholastic, literary, artistic, or career accomplishments, which, in my eyes, are far more worthwhile and lasting than any accident of beauty.

My mother and I were very close during my childhood. I was an only child and had *all* her attention. As I grew older we became more like friends than mother/daughter. When I had children of my own, she was a close and caring grandmother—very loving and involved with my children.

For forty-six years we had an almost ideal relationship, but when my father died it *drastically* changed. My mom expected me to step into my dad's place in her life and do everything he did, from handling her finances to maintaining her home to meeting her need for companionship to ease her loneliness. Her demands were unrealistic and I couldn't begin to fill my father's shoes. She was bitterly disappointed in me and began to whine, complain, and demand. I realized she was having trouble dealing with grief over the loss of my dad, and I *begged* her to get professional Christian counseling, but she refused.

Within a year, she developed serious health problems. She broke one hip, and then almost a year later, she broke the other one. It was after her second hip surgery that she developed a blood clot that killed her.

After forty-six happy years together as mother and daughter, the last two were awful. I am thankful that I had all those good years with her, but with all my heart I wish that we could have ended as well as we began.

No better than okay. She didn't understand my personal relationship with Jesus, so she didn't share on a very intimate basis. She didn't pray with or for me. She never wrote me a letter.

A tepid relationship. I love her but wonder if my feelings aren't out of obligation instead of my heart. I call her three to four times a week. I care what happens to her, but I think I somewhat lost respect for her for not standing up for herself against my dad.

I knew my mother loved me, but it was a distant relationship because she worked from early in my life until I was married. When I was born, my father was dying from high blood pressure and kidney disease. He eventually died from a stroke when I was two. Before his death, I believe my mom spent most of her time with my dad, and it was my grandmother who took care of me and nurtured me. I knew my mother loved me a lot, but she didn't express it emotionally. Instead, she showed it in practical ways. I needed to be emotionally close to her and to feel her love and approval, but I rarely felt it. Because my brother looked so much like my dad, the love of her life, she seemed to love him best, and I often longed to be a boy who looked like my dad so she would love me as much.

Strained at best. We never talk unless I call her. She only (sometimes) calls on major holidays to see if I'll make the hour-and-a-half drive to see her and the rest of the family. She never drives here unless my sister brings her.

Competitive, hateful, sad, disappointing, highly unfortunate, existing—she's still breathing. She was never interested in being my mom. We never did mother/daughter things together. She never noticed anything beautiful about me, never appreciated me; I never felt her genuine love.

My mother had a deep hatred for me. She seemed jealous. If I was thinner or prettier than her, she hated me and let me know it. She didn't protect me from my father's sexual abuse or physical violence—even when she knew it was happening—and she said it was my fault. I believe my mother had an affair with my uncle and he was my real father.

Mom and I were at odds with one another as far back as I can remember. I was an only child with a strong will, and it always seemed that I could not please her no matter how hard I tried. She was often negative and was a perfectionist. She held strong religious beliefs, and that always seemed to take the fun out of life.

Very distant. By choice I live twelve-hundred miles from my mother. When I call her she avoids real conversation by talking about the weather. As one of nine children I struggled growing up with my own identity. I felt loved by my dad but not by my mom.

There was no relationship. We lived in the same house, but that was it. She paid no attention to me but left me to fend for myself as far back as I can remember. She was unmarried when I was born. I didn't fit into her plans and never did. Taken from her at an early age, I was placed in a foster home. I was returned to her when she "proved" she could take care of me, but she didn't.

My mother was abused as a child, so she didn't hug us because she thought it was unnatural. I was born during a time when she was *very* depressed, so when she communicated there was no touch involved.

At age five, I was adopted because there were abandonment issues. I had created my own little world where I was safe from being hurt again. My adoptive mother was emotionally dysfunctional because of an incident when she was five. Because of the pain in both our lives there was no emotional relationship of any kind.

I was my mom's caretaker from when I was two; she was an alcoholic.

My mother and I have never been close. I don't remember her ever loving, touching, or kissing me except when I was going away.

Null and void. I feel no need for her in my life at present. She never really seemed to care about what was happening in my life and she still doesn't.

Close, but with some "understood subjects" off limits in conversation. There are definite boundaries.

My mother made it clear when I was younger that "she was *not* my friend, she was my mother." This, I feel, described a relationship with boundaries, which limited my comfort of opening up and freely communicating with my mother. I felt a distance and a level of need to perform as "her daughter."

At this time, my mother is not just my mother, she is my mentor, my confidant, and my best friend. I would say a daughter's relationship with her mother evolves and changes with age and maturity. During my preteen years I looked up to and adored my mother. She never really tried to be my friend during those years and at times was a tough, yet loving disciplinarian. During my teen years she tried to prepare me for going out on my own by giving me more responsibility for myself and also my finances. I cannot say how many times during this period I told her "I hate you!" (Thank God I have an understanding and Christian mother.) Between the ages of twenty to forty was a season of growth (and a lot of rebellion on my part). My mother and I reached the point where I would allow her to speak her mind to me, but then I would let her know if I disagreed with her (which was fairly often in my twenties and early thirties). With the birth

of my children (at twenty-eight and thirty) I started pro-
fusely apologizing to my mother. At each stage of my children's lives I have come to realize how difficult it is to be a
mother. After age forty, I settled into a deep respect and
admiration for my mother's faithfulness, not only to me, but
to her family and mostly to her Lord and Savior.

Superficial, not close. We talk about "surface" things, nothing of real depth. I don't feel like she would truly be there
for me if I needed her.

My mom was the major financial provider for our family.
Consequently, she was away from home a lot. This left me
with the main responsibility of keeping house and watching
over my younger sister. My mom seemed distant to me, and
we never really spent that much time doing things together.

As an adopted child, I consider the home in which I was
placed to be God's hand of blessing on my life. My older
sister was also adopted three years before me. My mother
was very close to my older sister and protective of her. At
times I felt their tight relationship left me out, even though
I believe my mother was not aware of this. As a result, I
spent most of my time away from home with my friends. I
didn't feel slighted, and to this day feel like I had a wonderful childhood.

My mother and I have a very good relationship. I consider
her one of my best friends, along with my sister. I have
numerous friends, but I generally only share some of my
deepest struggles with my mother and my sister. I know
they will hold me up in prayer, encourage me, and support
me in whatever way they can.

Mostly tense. She tended to be a rather nervous woman and
was ill quite a bit, but this was not surprising since she had

six children and raised us in a Third World country as a missionary family. I was the oldest and strong-willed, and she and I had some battles, though my father would not have allowed any outright rebellion or disobedience or disrespect. I can't say my mother and I were very close—I would not have "bared my soul" to her—and after I left home for college there was little opportunity for us to get to know each other as adults. The family was overseas for many years, thousands of miles away from me after I married and had daughters of my own. My mother died overseas many years ago and is buried there. She was the same age I am now— too young to die!

Very good. My mother considers me one of her best friends and I know that I can always look to Mom for support and advice. She doesn't push her advice on me but waits until I ask, which I appreciate. There have been times that I felt more like the mother, giving her advice and helping her to be patient with Dad, hoping things would not deteriorate into divorce. At that time she forgot, I think, that her husband was my father and was a little too open about their problems than I was comfortable with. But because I wanted to be a voice of good Christian influence on her, I toughed it out. They are now happier than they have ever been and I am glad I was there for her.

I am at peace now that she is deceased. Before, I was more her mother than she was mine. My mother had mental illness and struggled.

I love her, and she has always been there in a crisis. However, I wonder what it would have been like to learn things from my mother. She worked the second shift, so by the time we were home from school she was at work. Even on weekends she really didn't have much to do with us kids. My mother and father divorced when I was in kindergarten, so my mom raised seven kids on her own and I think she did a wonderful job. She does not have manners, does not clean very well, and doesn't know how to make a bed. I can't remember her cooking any meals or sewing, but when we were young, we did cleaning for neighbors and learned manners and how to clean while we were earning money; so even though she didn't teach us some of the things you need to know, we did learn them from someone.

My mother and I were very close once. We could talk to each other just about anything. But she was somewhat of a controller. Then I was married and had a daughter of my own and now we are becoming very distant. My mother is no longer a good listener and is too preoccupied with her own life, TV shows, quilting, and crocheting.

My mom is loving, nurturing, encouraging, and kind. She's not my best friend, as I hear some people describe their mothers, but she is a soft place to land. Recently, at the age of thirty-three, I have made the emotional break from my parents and been able to accept the fact that I have different convictions and beliefs than they do in some areas. It has been freeing and gratifying. I am so thankful for my mother's love.

She frustrates me at times with her need to still give me "motherly advice," but I've grown used to it over the years and don't let it bother me anymore. I know she only does it to be helpful.

Complicated. She's very self-centered. We get together at family things, but it's truly social.

Excellent! Mom had to be both parents to me, as she was a single mom. She did a great job of encouraging me and has always been there to listen and communicate. She is very generous; more than I could ever repay her. When I see single moms these days struggling to deal with the daily demands of a child, I realize just how much she did for me and probably gave up for me.

Identifying the Positives and Negatives

Before reading on, look back at your own answers to the survey questions, as well as the responses from the other women. Underline words or phrases that represent the positive and negative qualities you see in your mother. In the next chapter, we will ask you to use these phrases as you reflect on your mom, including your perceptions of her at three stages of your life: when you were a child, an adolescent, and now as an adult. If your mother is deceased, we'll ask you to evaluate her qualities through your last memories of her. All of this will help you discover and deal with your mother's influence.

Chapter Two

MEMORIES OF MOM

Life is made up of memories. Without them life is incomplete. We have no past; we have a form of amnesia. Over time, memories fade. They lose their sharpness. They may need photos or someone's reminder to activate them. But sometimes sights, sounds, and smells of an event can affect us more than we want. Anyone who has experienced a trauma such as an accident, a violent death, or abuse—maybe even seeing the World Trade Center towers crumbling in New York—have memories that when activated can immobilize us, creating panic or bringing back all the feelings we had when the event actually occurred.

You have mother memories. These pictures could be a reflection of who you are today. The mother memories you have contain the emotions you had as a child. That's all right. This emotion is as important as the memory itself. When we activate memories, we must be careful not to fall into the trap of using them to blame others. It's so easy to do this.

Memory is made up of bits and pieces from what we can remember of the past. Memories are not just factual events. It's more like a collage including feelings, images, perspectives, and fragments that we spread on a table and then piece together for our story. It becomes our life story. It is our history, and it's used to help us make sense of our lives. It doesn't matter who your mother was; it matters who you remember she was. What would you have said about your mother twenty years ago? Ten years ago? Five years ago? What would you have said about your life story twenty years ago? Ten years ago? Five years ago? You probably had different versions. There might be different themes and issues. Changes occur.[1]

One author put this in a helpful perspective:

> It is this very phenomenon that enables many reconciliations to occur. Old hurts, which seemed huge and insurmountable at one time, often recede to the back burner after a number of years as we gather new experiences in life; we frequently view the old ones from a different perspective when we are open to the changing landscape. Our lives can expand in ways that previously seemed impossible.[2]

"Time heals all wounds" is not necessarily true. Time by itself is not a healer. And depending upon what you do during that time, your pain could even grow if thoughts are fed and intensified. But when you put time together with distance and new life experiences, the intensity of some of the feelings and the desire for payment can be blunted. Some daughters mellow over time and want to move on while others become bitter and stuck where they are. They allow their mother to control their life and relationships even when they're seventy! It's interesting that they're angry at what she did or didn't do when they were young and how she dominated their life by this, but not letting go allows her to *continue* to dominate. Women end up moving through life not only lacking peace with their mother but also with themselves.

REINTERPRETING MEMORIES

How you view Mom today was shaped by what you collected and stored away as a child. But the memories were also interpreted by you as a child with a child's way of thinking. Sometimes what we see is marred by the way we need to see people around us. And all of this feeds your memories.

Dan Allender said, "Memory is to some degree a reconstruction of the past that is highly susceptible to erosion, bias and error. It is a mistake to consider one's memory completely accurate, no matter the level of emotional intensity or detail associated with the memories. We should maintain a tentative, open and non-dogmatic view toward all our memories."[3]

Memories start with an experience, but we often "update" them based on images formed and shaped by the intensity of emotions. Details are altered and some parts are reinforced and intensified while other parts are diminished. All the pieces go together and, for example, form your attitude toward your mother. And as an attitude forms, we naturally search for other memories to fit our attitude. Many discount what they thought were facts for a version of what happened or what they experienced. The authors of *How to Manage Your Mother* describe this phenomenon:

> When we begin to examine our recollections of our mother closely, we find that they are malleable. That is not to say that the original memories are false; but what we thought were the "facts" of our past may turn out to be only a version of what happened to us, a "take" on our experiences with our mother which we fixed in our mind long ago. As long as these memories stay fixed, we are locked into an attitude, a general feeling, a guiding image of our mother that makes it difficult to change our relationship with her today. But when we recall and reexamine our memories, we realize just how constructed they are by our guiding image. So they can be deconstructed, and when we do this, our feelings about the event and our mother can change also. This is why reconsidering our shared personal history with our mother can make an enormous difference to the way we get along with her.[4]

If you discover how your memories were shaped, it's possible to alter some of those memories, which can change your perception of your mother.

Discovering the Past

Some daughters have said the key to understanding where they are now in life is their memories. They say their past is controlling their present life. Perhaps there is another way to look at this. If you

STOP AND TAKE STOCK OF WHAT YOU THINK AND FEEL ABOUT YOUR MOTHER

grapple with what is occurring in your life at this time, the present, and take responsibility for it, perhaps what needs to be known about the past will become clear. As one writer said, "In that sense, *the past is the servant of the present*—and change in the present clears the way for whatever God wants us to know about the past."[5]

From time to time it will be important to stop and take stock of what you think and feel about your mother. Perhaps the question to ask is, "How did my mom affect my life?"

Throughout this book you'll be asked numerous questions. Some won't affect you at all while others could activate some intense feelings. Take another piece of paper and draw a circle like the one here:

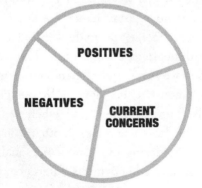

Divide it into thirds and label the sections: Positives, Negatives, and Current Concerns.

In the Positive section identify your mother's positive contributions to your life and her positive qualities. In the Negative section list what you think were your mom's negatives or shortcomings. In what way wasn't she there for you? If she died, abandoned you, or you didn't know her well, what were the benefits as well as disadvantages of her not being around? In the third area (Current Concerns), list your present-day concerns or problems with your mother. Write down whatever comes to mind as quickly as you can.[6]

EARLY RECOLLECTIONS

What's your first memory? How old were you? I've heard some amazing stories over the years, memories people have from age four, three, and even two.

Let's begin with your first memories.

My first three memories are . . .

1. _____

_____

2. _____

_____

3. _____

_____

My first memory I have of my mother is . . .

_____

_____

and I was _____ years old. As I think about this I feel . . .

_____

_____

My best memory I have of my mother is . . .

_____

_____

As I reflect on this memory I feel . . .

_____

_____

My worst memory I have of my mother is . . .

_____

_____

As I reflect on this memory I feel . . .

_____

_____

The last memory I have of my mother is . . .

_____

_____

As I reflect on this memory I feel . . .

_____

_____

Now list ten other memories that come to mind when you think about your mother. You may even want to use the questions that follow to spark possibly significant memories. Describe how these memories affect your life today.

1. _____

_____

2. _____

_____

3. _____

_____

4. _____

_____

5. _____

_____

6. _____

_____

7. _____

_____

8. _____

_____

9. _____

_____

10. _____

_____

Remember when . . .
Your mom gave you your best present?
You laughed the hardest at something your mom did or said?
You were the most upset with her?
You never wanted to talk to her again?
You were most proud of your mom?
Your mom was the most proud of you?
You discovered a secret about your mom?
You felt sorry for your mom?
You first rebelled against your mom?
You felt embarrassed being with your mom?
You said something to her you wish you could take back?
You shocked your mom with something you said?
You first shared a spiritual experience together?

What do these memories tell you about your mother?

Who would you be without these memories? Memories are part of our life stories. But it's not just the memories that make up the story; it's our response to them.

If your mother was somehow absent from your life, you might not have many firsthand memories of her. Perhaps the primary source of information about your mother was your father. What is the impact of that information upon what you believe and feel about your mother? Think about what you've heard over the years from your father (or someone else). Has it strengthened your feelings for her or weakened them? What are ten comments you heard about your mother?

1. _____

_____

2. _____

_____

3. _____

_____

4. _____

_____

5. _____

_____

6. _____

_____

7. _____

_____

8. _____

_____

9. _____

_____

10. _____

_____

Now go back and indicate which comments were positives and which were negatives. In chapters 7 and 8 we will talk more about making peace with a mom who was emotionally or physically absent from your life.

IMPERFECT PARENTS

All of us are flawed. There are neither perfect parents nor perfect daughters. We all have a condition called *sin*. And God loves us in spite of it. He wants us to grow spiritually, and in doing so we can become emotionally and relationally healthy. If you have set either parent on a pedestal, don't. Never idealize a parent, because it leads to disillusionment and hurt.

Hopefully others could see the strengths in your mom and focused on this in your presence. A healthy family is one in which both Mother and Father build each other up, whether the other spouse is absent or present. Can you remember statements in which your father praised your mother in front of you? Did he ever criticize her in front of you? Did he ever try to get you on his side on some issue? Were there many disagreements between the two of them over disciplining you or how to raise you? Which one (if any) felt they were the expert? Who ran the house, or was it shared leadership?

Why should we bother with memories about our mother? That's the past, and the apostle Paul said, "Forgetting what is behind . . . I press on" (Philippians 3:13–14). That's true. But to forget past pain we need to *make peace with our past*. What happened in our past does count. Too many people deny the impact of their past, and this only limits their healing and moving forward. As your mother memories unfold and are identified, life changes can occur. These memories affect the way you relate to others, how you see yourself, and even how you perceive God.

Later in this chapter we'll present an exercise to help you process your memories objectively and start to move forward. First, though, are examples from our survey of how women feel they have been influenced—negatively and positively—by their mothers and past experiences.

Negative Influences

The sense of abandonment—of physically watching her walk away from me and my siblings—is something that I may never completely recover from. It has affected my sense of confidence in everything I do and am. I am learning to deal with this because I am more aware of the ways this has so deeply impacted me. Commitment is also somewhat of an issue for me—both at work and in relationships.

She turned me off to marriage. I swore I would never be "controlled" by a man.

She's the denial queen. She denies every horrible thing that ever happened: the beating and especially the incest.

I have adopted every critical, condemning, and negative thought in my daily thinking. I am never good enough for myself, and this has caused severe depression. I get better at replacing these thoughts each passing year.

My mother has made me feel like a piece of nothing. She has caused me to seek love from people who could never provide the love I need. There is incredible pain in my soul; incredible disappointment, loneliness, ultimate unworthiness. I hide myself, feeling ashamed and helpless; never feeling good about myself. I have felt I was missing her love through all of my life.

I made up my mind early on that I would be everything she wasn't. I hated everything about her.

Since I did not have a relationship with my mother, I did not know how to relate to my daughter. I was there for her physically but not emotionally. I didn't realize this until just a few years ago when my daughter became very hostile toward me over a misunderstanding. Her actions were toward someone she disliked very much (me). I was shocked because I didn't have a clue.

My mother never was able to teach me the realities of life or how to deal with them because she never learned them.

I grew up trying to win her love. It was impossible because she put up a wall toward me. I grew up always feeling I could never do "enough." This carried into my adult life, and at fifty I am just finally getting free.

She has little control over her tongue and tone of voice. Raised in a home like this has made it challenging not to repeat bad communication behaviors. She's a strong person, I think, and I am as a result.

I now know that my mother hates me. She turned on me and accused me of things so untrue—things a person should never say to a family member. She is mean. There is very little she doesn't criticize about me even today. She hates my hair, I'm too fat, I don't do anything right, I steal from her, I mess in her business, I lie. These things are *all untrue* and I am the only one she says these things to. I am also the only child that does anything for her. I am still having a hard time coping with this. I have cried for months now. Without Jesus I would not and could not have made it.

I have low self-esteem and horrible body image issues. I don't like to ask for help because I don't trust others much. My communication skills are bad, but I'm working on this every day.

One way she shaped my life is that I am very private. I don't tell people personal things. Growing up—and even when I got pregnant at nineteen—everything was about my mother. I remember finally getting up the courage one night to tell her I was pregnant only to wake up to the sound of her on the phone telling people that her daughter was pregnant. That Sunday she told the entire church and yet never once spoke to me about it.

I've had to work hard to lose her negative habits (e.g., guilt trips and self-centeredness). I've made a point to have more fun with my children and make positive memories. I've become a good listener.

At times I have seen my mother have a critical spirit toward others. Unfortunately, this has tended to rub off on me, and I have noticed that I, too, can be critical of others. I have really prayed about this area and believe God is working in my life to help repair this.

She instilled in me a sense that there is only one right way to do a lot of things, and this has caused me to butt heads with my husband about stupid things. Also, I have inherited her tendency to judge people and complain about things not being fair.

Like her, I tend to get a bit grouchy when I am lacking in sleep, and I share nearly equal disinterest in all things financial and mechanical. I also feel great emotional trauma over slight family rifts and geographical separations at times, knowing how hard these things are on her too.

My need to be "perfect" and have everything around me "perfect." I put a lot of pressure on myself, which sometimes frustrates me and carries over into my relationship with my husband. I expect him to do things the way I think is best, which isn't always fair.

She has always been a worrier, and I think some of that obsessiveness started to rub off on me when I graduated from college and got married. My sister and I have often talked about how we can feel like she is our mother, yet have no distinct emotional attachment to her. We have both vowed to be involved with our kids and to communicate with them and love them.

Because of her I have trouble trusting myself and others. I am often paralyzed by fear of failure and guilt over past failures. I suppress my emotions and my ability to hope, to dream about the future, and to set goals in order to avoid failure and pain. I isolate myself emotionally from others. I understand intellectually that I have worth, and I can see that there are things I am good at, but I still struggle to feel like I'm worthy of good things, happiness, success, love.

Positive Influences

I learned from her mistakes. I have always had a relationship with God. My mom nurtured me when I was young. She was a single mom and always working. I knew I would marry a man who loved God and was unlike any other man I knew, so her negative experiences turned to positive ones for me.

She influenced my life because early on she met my emotional needs. I know what it is like to experience unconditional love, nurturing, discipline, etc., and I also know what it is like to lack them. She has taught me to work hard both in my job and life in general. She has taught me how to dig deep and how to fight. She has also taught me not to settle in relationships. I have also learned to appreciate my mom's mistakes. I see and know the consequences of unwise decisions; I live the ripple effects of her choices.

She is very creative, and I believe that any creativity in me has come from her. Seeing all the clutter and disarray in her house has made me careful about how I keep mine.

She taught me by example how to be a good mother, how to nurture and have fun with my children. My mother also taught me how to be a good hostess, how to care for my home, how to decorate, and how to make the holidays special. She influenced me to believe that marriage is for life; even though she was unhappy in her marriage with my dad, she remained faithful to him. My mother also shaped me academically by pushing me to get good grades and go to college and have a career.

She was a wonderful example, and when I was in the seventh grade she became a good example of a Christian. She was fair and firm but kind; she was smart and attained great success as a career woman. She sacrificed for me and was very family oriented.

Her love for me and others has made me a more loving person. Her love for God helped me grow in godly knowledge and love for Him. She had a servant heart for the "bums," as we called them in the '40s, and I would come home from school and find her feeding them meals. I learned from her example that we are *all* God-created.

If I had not been left so alone and distant from my mother, I might not have been so desperate to reach out and find

God. I prayed faithfully for my extended family members and in time I was able to lead various family members to the Lord before they died. I believe that God used my mother's pain, depression, discouragement, and stress to bring me to faith in Jesus Christ.

The most positive thing was her influence in my walk with God, which is probably the most important part of life to impact.

My mother is extremely honest and moral. I have tried to live my life in a way that would make her proud. I always think of her when put in a situation that might compromise my values, and this helps me to make the best decisions. I grew up in a home where no one smoked, drank, or swore. This is an environment I'm comfortable in and I was fortunate to find a husband with the same upbringing.

WHO AM I?

There are various steps you can take to change what occurred or didn't occur in the past—all of which has brought you to where you are today. Some women have shared that even though they don't look like it, they feel their growth as an adult was stunted because of what happened to them as a child. Some say they feel like a child in an adult body. Many who were hurt learned to develop layers of protection. As one woman said,

I'm like a walking onion. I know it's a weird word picture, but I have all these layers of protection I wrapped myself in. That's what you find on an onion—layer upon layer of onion skin. And when I was growing up, much of my energy went into making sure I was safe. But I became so safe I lost sight of who I was as a person. I'd like to "meet me," if you know what I mean, and discover who I am and who I could have been.

47

When I heard this last phrase it struck a chord. Many of the adult daughters I've talked with over the years have said the same thing: "I wonder who I could have been . . ."

Here are suggestions that can help you objectively process your memories and discover who you are, who you could have been, and what you can do now in order to more forward.[7]

First, when is the last time you looked at photographs of yourself as a child? Find those pictures and select one or two at different ages. Choose those that really depict you at that age, and then ask yourself the following questions as you look at each picture. This might bring up intense feelings. If you can't answer the questions for a particular age, try to determine what happened at that age that is creating the blockage. Here are the questions. (Some are asked as if they are about someone else in order to help you become more of an objective observer.)

1. Where were you and what were you doing?
2. How did the child's mother respond to her at this age?
3. What was the most fun for this child at this time?
4. What kind of care and love is the child receiving at this time?
5. What kind of parenting did the child receive that was beneficial?
6. What kind of parenting did the child need that she didn't receive?
7. What kind of parenting did the child receive that was destructive?
8. What did the child learn about mothers at this age?
9. What could this child learn now that would fill in the gaps in her life and help her to feel more complete?

Now, having completed this for several ages, how would you summarize your childhood to someone else? Write a summary statement based on all the information gleaned from these questions.

If you discovered that you missed out on some things in your life at various ages, then you experienced losses. And in order to move on, it's important to grieve over those losses and eventually say good-bye to them. Then you'll be able to move on with your life.

As you look at the parenting you needed but didn't receive, in what way have you received that as an adult? And if you received it, did you accept it?

MESSAGES FROM THE PAST AND TODAY

Most of us have voice mail or answering machines. We want to make sure we don't miss any messages. We pick up the phone, hear a beeping tone, dial our code, and hear the words, "You have three messages." Some have call-waiting and will interrupt a conversation to answer so they don't miss the message.

There are messages, however, that some women wish would disappear: negative messages from Mother that were planted in the past yet surface today. Sometimes they're even heard in Mother's voice, the focus of the next chapter.

Chapter Three

MOTHER'S VOICE—
DO YOU HEAR IT?

Jenny perfectly described a common experience of women.

We have movies today about the whisperer—*The Horse Whisperer*, *The Dog Whisperer*, *The Ghost Whisperer*. Well, they need to make another movie: *The Mother Whisperer*. I can hear her right inside my head—I hear her when I dress my daughter, when I try something new, when I want to eat that dessert, when I want to spend a large amount of money. Oh, no one else can hear her, but I can. And it's strange: Mom didn't always say it verbally; it was the way she looked at me. I guess I've transcribed that into an audible whisper.

My mother lives in my head. She sits up there and programs what I think, what I say, and what I do. I'd like to find the Disconnect button and then give an eviction notice.

I received the ultimate insult the other day from my husband. I was correcting my daughter about something and he said, "Jenny, you sound just like your mother!" I was shocked. I stopped and looked at him, fuming. And probably because he was right!

Many daughters have never learned to manage their mother's

influence, which often exerts itself in the form of "Mother's voice." And even when that voice frustrates you, makes you want to move (or ship her) to Siberia, brings tears of dismay, creates heartbreak, and makes you dread the phone calls and visits, most daughters continue their relationship with Mom as it has been for many years. Some daughters find themselves shifting between being their mother's advocate to wanting to divorce her.

MESSAGES FROM TODAY

The messages of Mother were born in the past but can continue today. Do you hear them? Does her voice resonate in your head?

If your mom is still a part of your life, are your conversations uplifting and fulfilling, or just the opposite? One daughter said talking with her mom is like "picking my way through a minefield. One wrong step and I'm on a detonator and it blows up."

What about you? Have you ever shared an experience with your mom, only to be peppered with questions such as:

"What did you wear?"

"What did you eat?"

"What did you talk about?"

"Did you see anyone you knew?"

"What time did you get home?"

"What time did you get up?"

Are questions like these mildly irritating, an intrusion, or just a sign that Mom wants to be a part of your life? How involved is your mother in your life? Are you comfortable with this involvement? Many daughters say their mother is like a shadow, always breathing down their neck. And it doesn't matter whether she lives next door, in the next city, or three thousand miles away.

> I've worked very hard at school and in my profession to get where I am, but my mother doesn't think I can handle life on my own. It seems that I'm her whole life and always will be, and it's gotten much worse since my dad died. She doesn't know how to let up. She's always bringing food over to my apartment because she doesn't think I eat well

enough. Sometimes I come home and find she's cleaned my place "as a favor." She's even rearranged my clothes, furniture, and bathroom articles! When I asked her to stop she just cries and says, "What's wrong with a mother who helps a daughter she loves?"[1]

My mother is overly invested in my successes and failures whether it be in my career, mothering, or social standing. I think she's living her life through me. I always hear how much I've been given and all the opportunities I've had that she never did.

I'd love to say this to my mother: "Why do you say the things you do? Why is everything I do wrong? Why can't you treat me like an adult? What difference does it make to you if I don't become a nurse and what difference does it make to you who I marry? I'm the one who will be living with him. When are you going to let me go? Why do you act as if every decision I make on my own is an attack on you?"[2]

Some mothers are respectful. They call first, give advance warning they're coming to town, or ask if the time is convenient. They don't call several times a day—or worse yet, at night—and they don't offer advice unless requested. When they say, "This is just a suggestion," they mean it. Other mothers invade and have no regard for your time, privacy, or boundaries.

DOES THERE NEED TO BE A RESETTING OF THE BOUNDARIES?

Are you comfortable with the distance you have with your mother, or does there need to be a resetting of the boundaries? The ideal is having a relationship in which each of you feels neither too close for comfort nor too far apart for meaningful contact. The best illustration we've heard comes from the realm of nature. In a forest the seeds that have the best opportunity to grow are those that land neither too close nor too far away from the mother tree. If they're too close they don't receive enough sunlight. They also risk being exposed to toxins that may come from "maternal" roots or leaves. But if the seeds fall too far away, they lack the shade they need and are more likely to be impacted by other dangers since they're unprotected and vulnerable. Trees can't select where they take root, but you can shift your position if you're in a danger zone.[3]

Setting Boundaries

A boundary is a border that defines our personal territory, both physical and emotional. When a boundary is crossed illegally, there are problems. When it's done properly and under an agreement, there is harmony. Emotional boundaries are often violated in mother/daughter relationships and create feelings of vigilance. One author said that if you find yourself grinding your teeth when Mother is around, you probably have some unresolved boundary issues.[4]

Does your mother invade your space? You know, come over to your home and just take over? If so, have some other task for her to do. Let her know it would be helpful for her to work on another project while you continue doing what you are doing. If you have to repeat this request five times, do it. You're in charge of you and your home, so be sure you take charge. And it doesn't matter if Mom doesn't like what you do. In fact, give her permission to be thrown by your new responses. If you want to change your relationship, you need to break set patterns. Do the unexpected. Create a game plan so when Mom drops in you know what to do.

Have you thought about how much time you want to spend with your mother? How often do you see each other? How often do you *want* to see each other? How often and how long do you talk on the phone? How long do you *want* to talk on the phone?

Have you ever said, "Mom, that wouldn't be convenient. Let me get back to you when I have some time," or "Mom, I'd like to but I have something else scheduled"? If she responds, "Well, what is it?" or "Can't you change your plans?" don't respond to these questions. By giving her an answer you hand her control. Simply repeat your original statement, and then go on to something else or say, "Let's look at another time." Don't respond to jibes or "poor me" types of statements. Don't get hooked into those games. Here are some other boundary-setting statements:

- "Mom, I can only talk for a few minutes right now."
- "Mom, I'll call you this weekend when I have time to share all the details with you, which I know you want to hear."
- "Mom, some of this information I can share with you and some I can't. I'm sure you understand that." (This is especially helpful if Mom tends to bring up sensitive subjects again and again.)

MESSAGES FROM THE PAST

Certain approaches and strategies help when your mom's presence or comments invade your life today. But what about unhealthy messages that were planted in your past that still have an effect?

When we're young, it's easy to take what our parents say as the gospel truth. Children receive an incredible range of messages. Some are wonderful while others wound:

"You're no good."
"You're not pretty and never will be."
"You'll always be fat."
"You'll never measure up."
"You'll never please anyone."
"What you feel isn't important."
"You can't trust your feelings."
"You can do anything."
"You are such a special child."
"I am so proud of you."
"You will make some man so happy."

You see how these messages vary. I wonder what messages you're carrying around—ones you want to keep and those you'd like to erase.

Is there a woman alive who has not, at one time or another, felt influenced by the voice of her mother that she hears in her head? We find ourselves continually amazed by the authority of the "motherly voice" residing within grown women. Usually heard as an internal dialogue between herself and her mother, a daughter can experience her mother's voice as soothing, comforting, and emotionally grounding. At other times, however, it can agitate, criticize, demean, or paralyze.[5]

Mom's voice becomes embedded within the daughter's heart and mind, especially when the messages are critical, ridiculing, or reflect disinterest. A negative message has the power to override a daughter's positive feelings about herself. And the more this occurs, the more it's embedded in the daughter's memory retrieval system. It has future consequences because it affects how a grown daughter will raise her own daughter. The authors of *Mending the Broken Bough* described it in this way:

- In order to feel worthwhile, a daughter needs to feel accepted and valued by her mother.
- A daughter's emotional response to her mother's behavior toward her will be experienced as both the inner "mother's voice" she hears and her own internalized self-image.
- If the messages a daughter receives from her mother are experienced as critical and/or judgmental, they will have the long-term effect of eroding a daughter's sense of well-being.[6]

Some mothers and daughters are so connected and immersed in each other's lives that the emotions of one become the emotions of the other. Deborah Tannen described this in *You're Wearing That?*

I always felt as if there was a wire running from my mother's chest to mine, because her emotions were directly transferred to me. When I called her, I knew from the way she answered the phone which emotion I was about to absorb.

If her intonation went up as she said, "Oh, hello, sweet-heart, how *are* you?" my spirits lifted. But my spirits sagged if her intonation was flat as she said, "Hello. How are *you?*" I now know that I'm not the only woman attached by this wire, and that the wire can conduct current in both directions.

The invisible wire that transfers emotions from one to the other also accounts in part for why many women do not want to tell their mothers about what's going on in their lives—especially about anything major that might be worrisome, like significant illness or problems at work. I was quick to tell my mother of small misfortunes, in order to receive the balm of her concern. But I did not tell her of serious problems, because if I did, I'd be sure to hear from her the next day, "I was up all night worrying about you." My problems became her problems, and I did not want to cause my mother to lose sleep—or to have to shift from seeking comfort to providing it.[7]

Take a few minutes and reflect on the messages you've received from your own mother.
Messages from Mom I want to keep:

1. _____

2. _____

3. _____

4. _____

5. _____
Messages from Mom I want to erase:

1. _____

2. _____

3. _____

4. _____

5. _____

And so, the question becomes, "How do memories of your mom and her messages affect you?"

Some of your Mother messages may be labels, and they've stuck. But do they need to be stuck? Are they really true? It could be that messages have been distorted in the remembering process. Some may be inaccurate, or what was said to you wasn't the truth. It's hard for some to admit, since a mother is seen as such a powerful figure. But mothers can be wrong.

Self-Talk

Do you ever talk to yourself? It's okay—we all carry on conversations with ourselves; it's normal. In this self-talk are words about ourself, our father, mother, spouse, experiences, the past, the future, God. Most self-talk is instigated by memories, and it can contain messages that have been imprinted in our mind for years. (Sometimes these messages are even in the form of pictures flashing in our mind.) Many of our emotions are initiated and escalated by what we say to ourselves. The more emotion that is attached to an event, the more we tend to remember. Repeated sets of self-talk turn into attitudes, values, and beliefs.

Let's consider some additional messages that women struggle with:

"You can't do anything right."

"You'll never be attractive; you'll never find a man."

"You never were much good."

"Other people would never have gotten fired like you did."

"You're fortunate to get any kind of job."

"Who do you think would want you?"

"You're a failure."

Are these friendly voices? Not at all. They're actually your enemies. They're deceitful. They distort reality. They're nothing but lies. We don't know how much stronger to put it. If you listen to these you'll end up with a bucket of feelings that you'd rather throw out than anything else. They can make you feel worthless, depressed, humiliated, afraid, insecure, anxious, shameful, you name it.

Your feelings today are often linked to memories. What happened in the past can lock in your response to the present. Many emotional struggles could be tied to negative criticisms from your mother or others. Their mistakes from the past limit your present functioning as well as the future. Fortunately, you can change these messages, especially with God's help, but it will take some work . . . and courage.

The problem is, too many women are reluctant to examine the past and their relationship with Mom. One woman said, "I'm afraid to look too closely. I guess I'm afraid of what I'll find. I don't want to discover that what I've felt all along is really true. It's like I would be betraying my mother. And yet it would explain why I respond the way I do. It may lift the pressure I put on myself. But then I don't want to blame Mom either." Many women find themselves in a similar quandary. But looking back, discovering, and evaluating is the only way to make changes and make peace with your mom.

The Bible teaches that we change our living by changing our thinking. "Do not conform any longer to the pattern of this world, but be transformed by the renewing of your mind. Then you will be able to test and approve what God's will is—his good, pleasing and perfect will" (Romans 12:2).

The simplest changes may involve some of the labels you've attached to events in your life. Remember, labels and messages can be changed. For example, if Mom rejected you, perhaps you say to yourself, "That was terrible. There must be something wrong with me." Now, we all know what believing these statements will do to you, so reread Romans 12:2 and then challenge each part of these false statements. "It's not terrible. It's unfortunate but not the end of the world. It's not that I'm defective. I have tremendous worth in the sight of God. It's too bad that my mother didn't have the ability to recognize this." You may have to do this numerous times until this negative belief is banished.

Go back to the sample messages that many women struggle

with. If any of these thoughts (or others) enter your mind, counter them by asking this series of questions. Let's assume your thought is, *I can't do anything right*:

1. What indicates this belief is true? Where is the evidence? If you were to ask three of your friends if this were true, what would they say?
2. What's another way of looking at this situation? An alternative response? You could make a list of what you're doing "wrong," but for everything you list you need to write down two things that you've done (or are doing) right in your life. You'll be amazed at the result.
3. If there is truth in your belief, what do you want to do to correct it? You're assuming you can't do anything right. For the next day let's assume you can't do anything wrong. What would that be like? One woman said, "It was ridiculous," but is it any more so than the other assumption?

Let's consider our common negative messages and put each one in perspective:

"You can't do anything right." A different perspective: "Sometimes I don't do things well, but most of the time what I do is quite good."

"You'll never be attractive; you'll never find a man." A different perspective: "Some days I look good and some days so-so—sort of like everyone else—and there are men who do care for me."

"You never were much good." A different perspective: "I'm not perfect and never intended to be, but I have a number of positive qualities. God knows me, loves me, has sacrificed for me, and I am worth His attention. In His sight I am really somebody."

"Other people would never have gotten fired like you did." A different perspective: "I have held other jobs that went well, and plus, plenty of others have been fired. It was a good learning experience."

"You're fortunate to get any kind of job." A different perspective: "I am grateful for having a job and I am qualified for a number of jobs."

"Who do you think would want you?" A different perspective: "Many people will want to spend time with me and already do. And when it comes to work, I can find a number of opportunities."

"You're a failure." A different perspective: "Mistakes are learning experiences; they create valuable lessons. I may fail at some things, but that doesn't mean I'm a failure as a person."

Do you get the idea? It's all about talking back to the old messages, those old lies.[8]

RULES TO LIVE BY?

Many messages you may hear in your mom's voice are actually "rules" she taught you. Some are good, others not so good—some are healthy and others are not so healthy. They can be discovered by listening to your "shoulds" and "oughts." Perhaps it was your mother who has taught you what and when you should eat, what nights you engage in certain activities, what you say to others in certain situations, how you arrange your kitchen, the way you respond to men, etc.

Rules are in place for several reasons. Some reflect your mom's fears, some are there to protect, and others were given in the hope that you would experience the best in life. Some rules were handed down from your mom's mom. You may be able to identify the times and places you first heard certain rules. Some were heard again and again, so it's no wonder they found a place in your belief system. But you also learned some rules by observing your mother—what she did and didn't do. They weren't taught verbally but were more absorbed. You overheard conversations and watched how Mom responded in various interactions. From this you might have learned:

- Which subjects should be discussed and which were off-limits.
- When it was appropriate to discuss certain subjects and when it was not.
- Whom to associate with and whom not to.
- What your family would do or wouldn't do.
- How you were supposed to act around men.
- How you were supposed to act around other women.
- How you were supposed to feel about school.
- How you were supposed to feel about work.
- How you were supposed to feel about yourself.
- The way you were supposed to act at certain functions.

Here are some of the "rules" daughters shared with us:

Your husband is the only one who can make decisions in the home—women have no say, opinion, or thoughts. Do as men say. They must be treated as kings. I've totally rejected these rules since my marriage. I've learned through my husband that my thoughts do count. I have an opinion and he wants to hear it. He helps me with 50 percent of the household chores. My mother still disagrees with this even after my seven years of marriage.

Never have women friends—you can't trust them. Many of my friends are older women whom I've accepted as my mentors, and I have learned that I can go to them for wise advice.

She is not aware she taught me this: *Divorce not an option; be picky when picking your husband; and relax, don't be stressed out all the time.*

If you are asked to help, always say yes. My mom stayed at home with us, but she was always busy with church or helping out at school. Sometimes she would be asked to help someone and she was angry and frustrated and sometimes she got upset with my sister and me. I always thought it was so crazy for her to be doing something nice for someone and yet angry while doing it. Now that I'm an adult, I find myself saying yes when I shouldn't, and if I say no I feel guilty.

1. It's a funny one. She said, *"If he's a bad kisser, he'll be bad in bed."*
2. *Always be there for your kids.*
3. *Marry for the right reasons.* I watched her and my dad's relationship. It's sad the way they treat each other.

1. *Don't litter, not even a little.*
2. *If you can't do something right, don't do it at all.*
3. *Pray about it!*

1. She used to say that I should hitch my wagon to a star. *You may not reach your highest dreams, but think how far you will go when you reach for that star.*
2. *It is important to be a lady at all times, whether you work and compete in a man's world, or if you face hard times, or when others are unkind and rude to you. Being a lady means behaving properly at all times, being feminine, polite, kind, generous, forgiving.*
3. *Being honorable is also important. This means being honest, fair, keeping your word, being willing to make the best of a hard situation, doing a job well, being loyal, and being a friend. Helping and standing beside family members in need is also important.*

As you think of your mother's rules, were they positive or negative? Most daughters have heard more negative rules than positive ones. Is your adult life under the shadow of unhealthy rules learned in childhood? It might be hard to even recognize the impact of these rules. Sometimes you stumble on a rule when you feel guilty, tense, irritated, or anxious for doing something seemingly normal. You're confused over your reaction and wonder where the feelings are coming from.[9]

It can be especially difficult to identify the rules that were "caught" rather than taught directly. Some women have found help by talking with their mother about her rules and what they meant to her. If you bring up the subject with your mom, though, know that she might not even be aware of the rules that were passed along.

SHE MIGHT NOT EVEN BE AWARE OF THE RULES THAT WERE PASSED ALONG

Genevieve told us: "One day I decided to list the rules I had heard from my mother when I was growing up. I was surprised by how many I remembered. I laughed at some of them, but others created irritation because I thought they still influenced my life. I decided to talk with Mom about them. It was interesting. She didn't remember all the rules that I did, and she called them suggestions rather than rules. I learned more about Mom in that discussion than practically any other interaction before. I thanked her but also let her know that some of the rules were helpful while others I discarded. She smiled and said she had done the same with her mom's rules."

Trudy decided on a different approach. "There's no way I would discuss Mom's rules with her," she said. "That's what we fought over most of the time when I was growing up. It's not worth bringing up—she felt she was right and that's that. I'm careful about what I bring up with her. I'm just trying to get those old tapes out of my mind. I just keep telling myself it's all right to create my own rules for life."

What rules from your mother are you thankful for?

_____

_____

What rules do you wish had never been given?

_____

_____

What rules are still guiding your life?

_____

_____

What rules would you like to evict from your life at this time?

_____

_____

How will you do this? (Complete this after finishing the chapter.)

_____

_____

LIVING BY NEW MESSAGES

In both the movie industry and the publishing industry there is a process used with scripts and books to bring them up to the best level possible. It's called rewriting. And it's in this process that mistakes and misinformation are corrected.

If you want to change messages or rules from the past, focus on what you want different or new rather than what you don't want. Write down any rule you don't agree with and simply rewrite it how you want it to read. Be sure the rule is healthy and adds to your life. As you reframe your rules in a positive way, consider these last questions:

1. Is the rule still in my life at this time because of my mother or because I've kept it there?
2. If this rule hadn't come from my mother, how would I feel about it?
3. If I change the rule how will it affect:
   (a) What I think about my mother?
   (b) How I view myself?
   (c) My life in general?[10]

Some people don't think it's possible to change the unhealthy messages they live by, but I've seen it work. Women have said, "I can't do it," but they can. And you can, too. You can learn, practice, and change.

Your thoughts are not your own. Your mind, like the rest of you, belongs to God. This truth, expressed in Romans 12:2, was presented earlier in the chapter. Other parts of Scripture teach us that our thoughts can change. In Philippians 4:8 we are told what to think about: "Finally, brothers, whatever is true, whatever is noble, whatever is right, whatever is pure, whatever is lovely, whatever is admirable—if anything is excellent or praiseworthy—think about such things." The power to do this comes through a personal relationship with Jesus Christ. This is how the reality of peace in our lives is finally realized. In Ephesians 4:23, Paul talks about being "made new in the attitude of your minds."

When you pray, ask God to renew your mind. Keep track of every unhealthy message from the past, challenge them, and ask God to purge your memory banks of these messages. Your goal is to realize that God, through the power of His Holy Spirit, gives each person the ability to picture things in the way He pictures them. Every person needs a transformation of the mind, to have the mind of Christ.

Dr. Lloyd Ogilvie, former chaplain of the U.S. Senate, says, "Each of us needs to surrender the kingdom of our mind to God." This is an opportunity for you to change messages that are keeping you stuck.

So can your messages change? Yes. Can your life change? Yes. Can your relationship with your mother change? Yes.

Chapter Four

MOTHERING STYLES

Not only do mothers come in all shapes, sizes, and personalities, but they have differing mothering styles. Your mom may have approached her mothering with a depth of knowledge and understanding equal to a PhD in motherhood. Others may have been terrified at the prospects of being a mom. Or your mother may have been the oldest of eight children, which means she helped raise a number of children before you came on the scene. Your own birth order affects the kind of mothering you receive as well. Every mother experience has its own sense of uniqueness.

How did your mother "mother" you? A strange question? Not really. Yes, all mothers "mother," but in this chapter we will describe nine main approaches to mothering and their usual results. Understanding your mom's parenting style will hopefully help your perspective on the relationship you had and the one you want. For now, though, reflect for a minute. If you had to describe the way your mother mothered you, what would you say? How would you describe it?

_____

_____

WHAT DAUGHTERS WANT
We don't know many daughters who don't want their mother in their lives. But they want a healthy, loving, and peaceful relationship.

They want their mother to "be there" for them. And many moms have been, judging by the following responses to our survey.

As a little girl, my mom was always there for me. She was a stay-at-home mom who worked alongside my dad on our family farm. I remember coming home from school many days and she would have just baked cookies, or supper was in the oven. I remember thinking that this was the best ever. I loved that she was always there. I knew what security and stability were back then. Needless to say, when she left, all of this changed and the void was huge!

When I was very young, she used to cook wonderful meals from time to time. She made sure we had every toy there was. Christmas at our house was extravagant, even though we had a very middle-class income. She always let us have a variety of pets too. I loved that.

She was a warm, safe person for me. She was kind, gentle, and generally fun to be with.

I think it has only been in the last few years that I feel my mom has or really is "there" for me in an emotional sense. It has taken me a very long time to realize that my days of the "milk and cookies" mom are long gone.

I always knew she loved me, though I never remember her saying so. Along with my father, she provided meals, clothes, and a house.

Mom cooked and we ate together. She cleaned house, made sure we were dressed properly, made us costumes, helped with homework, made treats, played games, and did family devotionals, including hymns.

She took me out of a family setting that would have been

disastrous and gave me opportunities I would never have had.

She was my cheerleader, encouraging me to dream, to go for those dreams. She was always ready to care for me when I hurt, and she wanted me to experience as much as I could, e.g., dancing, singing, sports . . .

She was always home when I was. She brought other children home from church so I would have playmates. She took me with her everywhere. I could tell her everything and she always answered my questions.

When I presented her with one of my *many* situations, she always made me feel like she was on my side. Then she would slowly insert perspectives about the situation from the other side. Fifteen minutes later, I had empathy for the person that I had hated (usually a teacher or girl at school).

Mom has been there for me in every way possible! Putting up with me, advising me, praying for me. I was in a very abusive marriage that dissolved. I was anorexic and had little or no self-esteem whatsoever. My mother came to my apartment daily, for what seemed like months, and made me look in the mirror and tell myself "I am a worthwhile person" until I finally started to believe that maybe I was. Even when my faith slipped and I turned away from it for a season, she never gave up on me.

She was everything I wanted my mother to be at the time. She was an old-fashioned stay-at-home mom, always there when I came home from school for lunch and always there when I came home after school.

My mom was there for me in countless ways. She is a very hardworking woman who always kept a beautiful home environment for our family. She never took time to relax (although we tried to coax her). She was always cooking, cleaning, ironing, working, serving, counseling, and ministering to people in our church and neighborhood, etc. She was always reliable and faithful to support me in all my school endeavors. She planned many fun and creative birthday parties for me. I often saw her studying her Bible and preparing for Bible studies she was involved in. The Lord is the most important thing in her life, and much of her time is spent serving in some way.

STYLES OF MOTHERING

In our research into mother-daughter relationships, we found that several writers identified "types" of mothers or mothering styles. Some of these classifications can be helpful because they give you a framework to describe your mother and also can help you realize you're not the only one in this situation. Be aware that some descriptions are extreme; your mom may exhibit or operate in degrees of a certain style.

The Self-Centered Mom

Most daughters care what their mother thinks. They want Mom's approval, even as an adult. Deborah Tannen describes the dilemma this causes:

A daughter wants to feel that her mother is proud of her, thinks she's okay. So any evidence that her mother's approval is less than total can be hurtful, and hurt can swiftly convert to anger. But how could a mother (or anyone) think her daughter (or anyone else she knows well) is perfect, doing everything right, every moment? All human beings could improve in some ways at some times, and people close to us are the most likely to see those ways. This means that the closer a mother is to her daughter, the more opportunities she sees for improvements—all the more because she wants to see things go well for her. But anything she says to help her daughter calls attention to perceived weaknesses, and that is the opposite of approval.[1]

Approval is especially difficult to get from a *self-centered* mother. Life revolves around her and her needs, even after the children grow up and leave the home. Many daughters pour so much energy into their self-centered mom that they end up shelving their own feelings and needs. Years later the daughter wonders why she tends to try to please everyone else and put herself in last place.

If you can't gain Mom's approval, you can either try harder or give up. A result of this is a daughter who struggles with low self-esteem. And if your relationship with your mother is insecure, you may find this happening in your other relationships as well.

Jean shared with us, "I try to limit the number of times I call my mother. It seems as if no matter what I share with her about what's going on in my life or my sister's, she doesn't end up talking about us and our lives. She turns the conversations back to her life. It's always about her! I want to feel like I count in her life for once. And the few times I mentioned this I paid dearly for saying anything. I feel punished. We get upset and then there's no contact for a while. I don't know how she feels, but I end up feeling terrible and guilty. Why does the world have to center around her?"

Mary said, "I feel my calling in life is to make my mother happy. It's true, when I was young I loved that response and smile on her face when I pleased her, but that was back then. Now is now, and she's grown harder to please. Do I need her approval? No. Do I want her approval? Yes and no. It's too costly on me now that I have my own life. But not only do I have Mom's voice in my head, I have another voice that says, 'Keep trying.' Am I an approval addict?"

Perhaps it's time to change the phrase, "I must have Mom's approval," to the following:

- "I don't need Mom's approval as much as I think."
- "I can't get Mom's approval all the time and that's all right."

• "It's all right for Mom not to understand or approve of all that I do."

Write these messages on a card. Whenever your old tapes begin playing, insert these statements instead. Take out your card and read them aloud. Do this as often as you need to. You're neither betraying your mother nor being a neglectful daughter. You're helping both you *and* your mother.

YOU'LL NEVER REMOVE ALL OF YOUR MOTHER'S VOICE

Here's a fact: You will probably *never* be the way your mother wants you to be. But your mother will *never* be the way you want her to be either! Can you fathom that? Your mother will never be the ideal mother you've dreamed of, and she may never even come close to it. Many daughters embark on a crusade to force their mother to change. It's doomed to failure. It's better to take that energy and invest it in building new ways of responding to her, creating healthy boundaries and refashioning new ways of viewing and talking to yourself. Perhaps you'll never remove all of your mother's voice, but you can moderate it and tune it down. Your approval is not based upon your mother's opinion. There's a much better way. It's God's opinion of you.

Judith Balswick gives some wise advice:

When we were children, we had little say in the way we were raised. As adults, however, we can choose to become all that God means for us to be. We can choose to make changes in our mother-daughter relationship, and we can also seek nurturance and affirmation from others. In God's kingdom there are no hopeless causes. But God leaves the choices to us.

The truth is, we always receive partial rather than total acceptance from our mothers and other family members. It is only in Christ Jesus that we are completely accepted just as we are. We are created in God's image and loved unconditionally by God. Knowing that, how can we refuse to accept ourselves? We are free to rest in the Lord, refusing to be ashamed of who God made us. We don't have to reach perfection in order to be acceptable.[2]

The Merged-Style Mom

A mother who "invades" your life has been classified as a *merged-style mom*. You are her life, according to her. Nothing is private for you. She wants and needs to know every tidbit of your life: where you go, who you talk to, what you do and see. And this inquisition doesn't happen just once every week or so. She may check in every day to get her "daughter's report." You're her life, whether you like it or not. It's as though you complete her. She can't bear the thought of your being independent from her or having a separate identity. This is a mother who lives for you. She's always available. Her life revolves around you, and when you are successful it is her success. When you fail, it is her failure too. This mother style puts an inordinate pressure on you to be a "good daughter." You don't want to fail because your mother would go into her martyr routine.

Some daughters were given a legacy of *worry*. Mother was a worrier and overly cautious. And when a child is young, she begins to believe, *If Mother believes it's something to worry about, it must not be safe, so I'd better worry about it too.* The passing of anxiety and apprehension from one generation to another is not a gift. It underlies a daughter's self-confidence and limits her risk-taking ability. Worry translates into overprotectiveness. It's living life as if "the worst could happen." Mother imposes rigid and set boundaries and limits her daughter's world.

If you grew up with the words *don't, can't,* and *watch out,* or her facial expression carried that look of concern, this was your mother. Mom wanted to play it safe in her life and wanted you to as well. Whatever you wanted to do, you were cautioned. Statement after statement curtailed what you wanted to do.[3]

We've both seen adult daughters who are too afraid to make adult choices and decisions without either checking with their mother or thinking, *What would Mom do in this situation?* They cave in to Mom's pressure. But we've also seen just the opposite, women who seem to think, *What would Mom say? I'll do just the opposite.* They rebel. It's the only way to demonstrate that the daughter is in control of her life. Unfortunately, some of the choices she makes aren't the best, and even if she knows this, it's better than letting her mother rule her life. But the problem is when you do the opposite of what your mother would say or want, aren't you still allowing her to control your decisions?

The Driven-by-Appearances Mom

Paula grew up with a *mom driven by appearance.*

Mom always had to look perfect, and it seemed like her purpose in life was to make sure I always looked good. But it was according to her standards, and was she ever a perfectionist! The time and money she spent on herself and me, making sure we were a "showcase," was ridiculous. I longed to have her say "I love you" and not look me over to make sure every hair was in place or my shoes weren't scuffed or I didn't look too fat or too thin. If she thought I was eating too much, she'd take the spoon out of my mouth. And this attitude stuck. I'm addicted to mirrors; I can't pass one without stopping to make sure "everything" is perfect. It was hard to please her and it's hard to please me. I've given up trying to get her approval with what I do. How I look is all that she cares about. And I guess I'm the same way. I guess that's why I've had some struggles with anorexia. I would have loved to have Mom accept me when I looked terrible, but it's not going to happen. She hardly lets anyone see her unless she's just stepped out of the showroom. Maybe that's why I've had such a hard time with my relationships with men. I don't know how to connect any deeper than looks.

The mother driven by appearances often transfers her insecurity to her daughter. That's the unfortunate side. The good news is it can be overcome.

The Competitive Mom

Some mothers are threatened by their daughter's accomplishments or life in general. This is the *competitive mother,* who wants to be the center of attention. No matter what you get, what you wear, how you do it, Mom will try to do it better. She has to be the top woman. If your mother is bothered by growing older and having her options in life diminish, it may enhance her competitive tendencies. Having a mother like this is a challenge. As the authors of *How to Manage Your Mother* describes, "Life with a competitive mother sounds almost as grueling as an Olympic marathon. The ability to endure and develop in spite of mother's agreed-upon place as front-runner is a challenge to be sure. Many a daughter alternates between frantically sprinting full out and competing avidly against her mother, then dropping back to applaud her at the finish line."[4]

The Neglectful Mom

Some mothers are *neglectful.* In some way they were distracted from following through with even providing parenting basics. These moms are often unresponsive to their children, so daughters have difficulty feeling loved or worthwhile.

Sue described her experience:

I wanted Mom to be there for me in so many ways. Sometimes my clothes weren't washed or she would forget an activity she was supposed to take me to. I wanted her to encourage me and cheer me on, but in so many ways she wasn't there for me. The emotional support I wanted and needed wasn't there and still isn't today. So if you can't get it from Mom you look elsewhere. I found my validation elsewhere, some good, some bad. Mom even brags that I'm so self-sufficient, I don't need her. It wasn't a matter of need. I was emotionally neglected. I didn't get what I needed.

It's natural for daughters to keep trying to get their mother to respond, to give them attention, to be there for them. Too often they end up wondering, *What's wrong with me? There's got to be something at fault in me and that's why Mom isn't coming through for me.*

The Nurturing Mom

EVERY PARENT
STARTS OUT
AS AN
AMATEUR,
AND MOST
HAVE LITTLE
OR NO
TRAINING

You might be getting the impression that all mothering styles are negative. Thankfully, there are plenty of *nurturing moms.* These are the mothers who give in a healthy way and respond in a way to help their daughters develop feelings of self-worth and competency. With a mom like this, there is a high degree of acceptance. She's supportive and encourages her daughter to develop her own identity. This isn't to say that she's perfect. The perfect parent is a myth because every parent starts out as an amateur, and most have little or no training to be a parent. And there may be occasions in a nurturing mom's life where the other styles show up, but not as permanent residents. [5]

The Martyr Mom

Daughters can be plagued by a *martyr*—their mother. Some mothers do have a hard life, or think they do, and make it hard on you by letting you and everyone else know. She reminds you in many ways how much she's sacrificed for you, her struggles, trials, or problems (some of which you caused). This mother employs guilt and is adept at controlling you. Susan said,

> I end up feeling responsible and guilty for every tough time Mom has. If I had the power and control she attributes to me, to give her all the grief she says or implies I've given, I'd be a superwoman. I feel like I'm always in debt to this woman and somehow I should make it up to her. But no matter what amends I make, she's like a bottomless pit.

Another example of the tactics employed by a martyr mom:

> My mother always made a big deal about all of us coming
> home for Thanksgiving. Last year, I won a contest at work
> and received a free trip to Mexico over the holidays. I was
> really excited since I could never afford a trip like this
> myself. I love the ocean and it was an incredible chance for
> me. This vacation sounded like a gift from heaven. When I
> told my mother, she looked like somebody just died. She
> looked down and her lip started trembling. She said, "It's
> okay, honey. You have a good time. Maybe we won't have
> Thanksgiving this year," which really made me feel terrible.[6]

The mother who blames her daughter for every ill takes a toll.
It exhausts you. You end up feeling emotionally uncomfortable
around her.[7] What does your mother want when she complains,
blames, or acts the martyr? Is there someone else she could complain to? Does she? Mother is probably trying to exact some payoff
by continuing this. And much depends on your response. You could
focus on her complaint, her issue of the moment, which you've
probably heard again and again, or you could hear the underlying
and true message—love me.[8] Martyr moms usually need an abundance of love and appreciation—and the word here is abundance.
Telling her "I love you" and "I appreciate you so much" when she
isn't in her martyr mode can go a long way.

The Critic Mom

The *critic mom* also falls under the ECM type. Translation:
Extremely Critical Mother. With a mother like this you feel as
though you're in Judge Judy's court, only the judge is also the jury
and you have no assistance whatsoever in defending yourself. This
mother is a flaw picker. Her life's mission is to pick apart whatever
you do and make sure you know how you messed up. It's true your
mother wants you to do your best, but the way she goes about
trying to motivate you is destructive to say the least.

Moms like this have the ability to throw a verbal hand grenade toward you. Your friends may be present, but it makes no difference to her. She cuts and dissects. Some moms do it with sarcasm and caustic humor. But unfortunately, the laughter is *at* you rather than *with* you. She may get other people to laugh as well, making an even higher price for you to pay.

Many critic moms are physically "frozen." When you reach out for a hug or embrace, she pulls back and comes up with some reason why she doesn't respond—usually it's because of some alleged problem or defect with you.

What she does and says activates shame and guilt. And most moms like this are very adept at taking explanations or protests of anger and turning them back on their daughters.

Victoria Secunda gives a fascinating description of the critic mom:

> The Critic is a woman in a state of constant dread, like a fugitive on the run—she is terrified someone will discover that she is really as unworthy as she accuses everyone else of being. The zeal with which she demeans her children is a desperate attempt to salvage, by comparison, some small shard of self-esteem. She conceals her tremulousness behind a wall of barbs and digs and nagging.[9]

Secunda suggests that such behavior is symptomatic not only of a battering mother, but of the psychologically battered "child" within the mother. Some daughters of ECMs end up with addictive personalities, whether it's to food or approval. It takes strength, persistence, and a new way of responding to break free from the grip of the critic.

The Controlling Mom

Another daughter described a different mothering style: "I call my mom 'boss lady' in my mind. She's got the final word, and her word is 'truth.' Any difference is a challenge to her dominion, and you'll pay the price if you cross her. She's a *controller*."

Mothers who are controllers have numerous characteristics.

They can be invasive, perfectionistic, even obsessive, critical, irritable, demanding, and rigid. They also have a mind-set that is anchored in cement. Their way is *the* way. This mother believes "my daughter owes me" and "I own her." Moms like this don't encourage; they push.

The controlling mom tries in every possible way to structure your life since she is the only one who knows best. She's a legend in her own mind. Part of the problem is she's good at what she does. She wants to be in charge. It's her way of feeling secure and she wants everything to be right for you. Some of them can activate guilt like you wouldn't believe.

The fear of not being needed motivates many controlling mothers to perpetuate this sense of powerlessness in their children. They have an unhealthy fear of the "empty nest syndrome," the inevitable sense of loss that all parents experience when their children finally leave home. So much of a controlling mother's identity is tied up in the parental role that she feels betrayed and abandoned when her daughter becomes independent.

What makes a controlling mother so insidious is that the domination usually comes in the guise of concern. Phrases such as "this is for your own good," "I'm only doing this for you," and "only because I love you so much," all mean the same thing: "I'm doing this because I'm so afraid of losing you that I'm willing to make you miserable."

Controlling mothers can create such emotional upheaval that daughters give in rather than experience the tirade. If you're a compliant daughter and have to make your own decisions in new situations, you probably ask yourself, *What would Mother do if she were here?* Once again, Mother controls.

There are times when the best choice is to be tenacious and stand your ground. The way in which you do this is important. You can be calm, definite, and persistent, even if the controller is loud and irate.

It also helps to use the broken-record technique. I realize that today with CDs and MP3s, there are some people who have never seen a vinyl record. Records came in three speeds—78, 45, and

33⅓ RPM. As the vinyl disc went around on the turntable, the needle would sometimes get stuck in a groove and the same words would be repeated again and again. This is where our phrase "broken record" comes from.

When you use the broken-record technique—repeating your answer, response, or request again and again, regardless of what the other person says—eventually the other person begins to yield. If you keep responding to a request with, "No, I will be unable to do that," you will stay in control.

When you're asked for your reasons (and you will be), just repeat the same statements. You don't have to give your reasons. If you do, you just give the controller more power. The broken-record approach does work! In time the controller may develop some respect for you because of your strength.

DISCONNECTING FROM THE CONTROLLER

There are times when your best move may be to disconnect. You don't always have to participate or cooperate with a controlling mother. Getting out of the situation by leaving, anticipating her moves, or eluding, ignoring, and not responding are some of the options you have.

Honesty Can Be the Best Policy

Another approach is called "leveling." It's simply being honest with the other person. It's an expression of the trait described in Ephesians 4:15: "Speaking the truth in love." One author suggests that this means speaking the truth in such a way that your relationship is better than it was before. It entails sharing what you think and feel about what Mother is suggesting. The sole purpose of this approach is to convey information—not to criticize, condemn, or change your mom. This can involve letting her know what you dislike, what you do like, and what you would prefer in the future.[10]

One of the best actions is to ask yourself, "What does Mother need from me that might lessen her need or desire to control me?"[11]

In the act of leveling you're trying to resolve the issue. The same principles we use in resolving conflict, listed below, will help when leveling with a controlling mother.

Some other common problems are when a mother is critical of where her daughter chooses to live, her decision to work or not to work, and her choice of occupation. This type of intrusiveness and criticism is really a violation of your integrity. Often this criticism expands throughout the years. It may appear especially when you're raising your child.

Mothers who are invaders tend to use the words "should" and "ought" excessively as they impose their standards on others. "Should" and "ought" imply, "I know better than you do and you ought to listen to me."

This problem has a fairly predictable outcome; it is called "shut out mother." Conversations become abstract and detailed plans are omitted from conversations. Avoidance is the order of the day, and this leads to greater deterioration of the relationship. Criticism and advice are more likely to be heard when "maybe" is substituted for "ought" and "should."

One young and courageous daughter, after hearing several "shoulds" and "oughts," shared with her mother the following statement:

"Mom, there are times when what you say makes sense, but for me the packaging of what you say could change just a bit and I would receive it better. Perhaps you could begin substituting the word 'maybe' for 'should' and 'ought.' And while you're learning, whenever you forget and use the old words, I will simply remind you by saying the word 'maybe.' Perhaps that will help." This is a positive way to handle a delicate situation.

If you can learn to respond to the facts of what your controlling or critical mother says, instead of reacting emotionally, you'll find yourself in control of the situation. Consider this interaction:

Mom: "Mary, I see that the children are playing outside and they're not dressed warmly enough again." (She and Mary have had a running debate over this for several years. Mary could reply with *any* of the following responses):

- *Mary:* "Mom! They *are* dressed warmly enough. I've told you that before!"

- *Mary:* "Oh, I think they'll be okay. Don't you have something else to do?"
- *Mary:* "You feel that the children should have some more clothes on? Thank you for letting me know that. When it gets cold enough I'll see to it, or I might ask you to call them in for me."

TYPICAL CRITICISMS

Following are three other typical statements a mother might make when visiting your home. Remember, these could be just statements of fact, or they could be statements made simply for the purpose of getting a response from you. After each statement, write down how you would respond.

1. "I see you have your refrigerator full of leftovers again!"
2. "You mean our granddaughter went out on a date tonight? Didn't you tell her that we would be dropping by?"
3. "You don't call or write me as much as you used to."

In each case, your mother would probably expect you to give an explanation or go on the defensive. But what would happen if you agreed with her statements? If you don't respond in the way that is expected, your mother may be forced to clarify what she really meant by the statement. Agreeing in principle with what someone has said does not mean that you change your own opinion or beliefs.

For example, what if Mary's conversation with her mother went something like this:

Mother: "Oh, I see you have your refrigerator full of leftovers again."

Mary: "Yes, I guess I do have some leftovers in there again."

Mother: "Well, some of them look like they've been in there for a long time."

Mary: "Yes, I am sure some of them have been in there too long."

You can see that this conversation could go on for some time without Mary committing herself to any change. She has little chance, also, of offending her mother.

Karen, a young woman attending a seminar, shared with me what happened to her. Whenever her mother would come over to her home, Mom would constantly check the house for dust and dirt. She was like a Marine sergeant who wears a white glove to inspect the barracks.

One day, after Karen had worked for hours cleaning the house and scrubbing the floor, her mother came for a visit. As she sat in the kitchen, her eyes spotted a six-inch section of woodwork next to the tile that had been missed. As she mentioned this to her daughter, Karen could feel the anger slowly creeping up through her body. Her face started becoming tense and red.

For the first time, her mother noticed this reaction to her suggestions. She said to Karen, "Honey, I can't really be of much help to you in anything else, but this is one thing that I can help you with." As she shared, Karen realized that her mother felt inadequate and useless around her, and this was the only way of attempting to feel useful and needed. Now both women have a better understanding of one another.

Avoiding Mom's Interference

Claire, a woman in her mid-thirties, had lived with her mother until she was married. She said she did this to save money, which makes sense. Sixteen months after the wedding, Claire and her husband, Ted, came into my office. Tension was developing between them over her mother. Claire felt her mother was continually interfering in their life.

Her mother phoned and visited often to contribute unsolicited advice. Claire tended to ignore what she said, but she did erupt with anger after she left. She refused to confront the problem head on but took it out on Ted as well as people at work.

After listening to them tell their story, I asked Claire, "Is the way you are handling this problem with your mother working?"

"No, not really," she answered.

"Then you really don't have anything to lose by trying a different approach, do you?" I suggested.

"You're right," she agreed. "I've got nothing to lose and a lot to gain. I really love Ted and my mother, but I feel caught in the middle. I know Mom's intentions are good most of the time. Perhaps I've added to the problem by not moving away from home sooner, and maybe I've relied too much on her advice. Now I've got to handle this situation. I do wish she would back off, but I haven't told her, have I?"

I offered a suggestion that has proved effective for most problems similar to Claire's. But it required that she adopt a new approach to the problem. She did not have to wait too long to try out her new plan. The next week her mother called her at home and gave some suggestions for her vacation.

Claire listened to her mom patiently, then said, "Mom, I need to share something with you. I become a bit upset when you make so many suggestions on what Ted and I should do. I realize that you love us and want the best for us. And I love you too. But now that I'm on my own and married, I need my independence. I enjoy some of our interaction, but too many suggestions bother me.

"I would like you to do something for me. I think it would work better if I called you once a week and you called me once a week. We can share what's going on in our lives. If you have a suggestion, please ask me first if I would like to hear your ideas on that subject. I think this way we will enjoy our relationship better."

Claire had prepared herself for several possible ways her mother might respond to this initial conversation. She could react with hurt. She did. She could become defensive and say she was just trying to be helpful. She did. She might withdraw by not calling for a week or two. She did. Or she could respond with statements of self-pity. She did.

In time, however, the relationship became much better. Claire had to repeat her request on two subsequent calls before it finally "took" with her mother. But it began to work.

How could *you* respond in a different way to your mother? Some women have said, "It's impossible. I've given up. All that works is either avoid her or get angry to get her to back off. But these are costly. It doesn't solve the problem." That's true. The question for you to consider is this: Is what you are doing working? If not, why keep doing it? There *is* a better way.

Your mother may be a critic or a controller or a perfectionist or a combination of all three. If Mom levels any criticism at you, don't deny it or get defensive or counterattack. Not in any way, shape, or form. Why? It won't work and doesn't solve anything.

Have you ever been in a heavy fog? We call this condition a fog bank. It's persistent, you can't see though it and it doesn't resist you when you penetrate it. It won't fight back. You can throw something through it and it doesn't fight back. You can't make it go away, so eventually you quit trying to make it disappear. You leave it alone.

When you're criticized by Mom and you offer no resistance, eventually her efforts will diminish. There's a name for what you can do—it's called fogging. But remember, you have to be willing to give up arguing with her or trying to convince her she's wrong. What you can do with what she says is threefold:

1. Agree with truth.

Mother: "Claire, you seem to be gone a lot in the evening. I called the last three nights until ten and no one answered."

Claire: "That's true, Mom. I have been gone several nights this past week."

Claire didn't deny nor give any additional information. It didn't cost her anything to just agree with her mother's observation. Think back on some of the statements your mother has made and how you could have responded in this way. It does work.

2. You could agree with the possibility that what Mom said is true.

Mother: "You know, if you're out so many evenings, you could wear yourself out and even get behind in keeping up that big apartment you have."

Claire: "You know, that is a possibility, Mom," or "I agree that I could get a little behind in keeping up my house."

3. You can also agree with the principle.

Mother: "You know, if you wear yourself down by being out so much, it could affect your work if you're too tired. It might be good to slow down your pace a bit."

Claire: "You're right, Mom. I wouldn't want my work to be affected, and if I start to get run down I'll stay home more."[12]

So how can you break free from your mom's interference?

Practice your responses in advance. Practice saying them out loud. Rehearse them. And when you're talking with her, practice following Scriptures in your interaction.

You know your mom. What are some of her usual criticisms? There are other ways to respond, which include asking a question requesting more information or clarification of each statement Mother says.

CRITICAL DAUGHTERS

We've talked with some daughters who feel so strongly about their mothers that they've said they would like to divorce them! However, as one author points out: "If this is the case, you're in a psychological prison. You can't really free yourself from her, but you can't really grow up either."[13]

Some believe that a mother should be an angel—perfect. Others see moms in the image of a "wicked witch." Both viewpoints create major disturbances. It's hard to have a relationship with anyone who is either perfect or wicked. Dr. Paula Caplan described a daughter's dilemma in this way:

But each of the two images is supported by a number of troublemaking myths or beliefs; for example, if we believe the "Perfect Mother myth"—that a mother meets all her children's needs—we feel cheated and angry when our mother doesn't measure up, and if we believe the "Bad Mother myth"—that it's wrong for a mother to stay closely connected with her adult daughter—we fear and resent our mother's offers of help or advice. These myths create avoidable problems that make dealing with the inevitable ones much harder.

The Angel/Witch, Perfect Mother/Bad Mother myths are rooted in a powerful tradition of mother-blame that pervades our culture. Most mothers are insecure about their performance as mothers and desperately need the approval of other women, including their daughters. Yet, tragically, as daughters we are taught to belittle the work of mothering and blame our mothers for almost everything that goes wrong. We too easily point out our mother's failings, without ever examining how much our negative view was shaped and intensified by the myths that lead to mother-blame.[14]

No matter how difficult you find your mother's behavior, it is important to remember that it is not her behavior per se that is causing emotional distress. It is the way you feel about her behavior. It is more difficult to deal with your frustration with her when you are not managing yourself very well. You need to feel emotionally secure to be able to overcome some of your frictions with your mother by seeing things from her perspective.

To be able to successfully confront your mother about particular issues without alienating her or treating it like a sort of revenge, you must feel confident and calm. Only when you are able to feel reasonably at peace with yourself can you deal well with the dynamics of your relationship with your mother.

ACCEPTING YOUR MOTHER IS A MOST IMPORTANT STEP TOWARD ACHIEVING A BETTER RELATIONSHIP WITH HER

At the heart of managing your mother, then, is being able to accept yourself with your own failings, for then you are more easily able to accept your mother, with all her flaws. And accepting your mother is a most important step toward achieving a better relationship with her.

Above all, know yourself. Only when you feel at peace with yourself can you deal well with the dynamics of the relationship with your mother. If you can accept yourself with your flaws, you can accept her with her flaws.[15] Unfortunately, this is probably easier said than done.

Mother-daughter relationships are packed with emotion. In the next chapter, we'll talk about a common barrier to healing: anger.

Chapter Five

A DAUGHTER'S ANGER

Jill, a thirty-four-year-old mother, could handle irritations some days, but other days she became a tinderbox, igniting at the slightest provocation. Without any thought, she'd rage at anyone in sight, regardless of their innocence or guilt. Later Jill told me why she was reacting in this way.

> For twenty-four years of my life I wasn't allowed by my mother to show anger or irritation. Any display was met with immediate disapproval and resistance. I felt over-controlled and repressed, but now I'm not going to hold anything back. If I feel it, I'm going to let it fly. Except I still don't show much around her. Everyone else gets it. My only concern is what if this gets worse over the years? Then what? I don't want it to. But I don't want to stuff it either.

Jill's actions are classic examples of a person who had been extremely controlled growing up but now responded by swinging from repressing rage to expressing it. Jill disliked the repression of her first two-and-a-half decades, but now she was actually afraid of the intensity of her anger. A balance hadn't been attained. "I guess I'm trying to make up for those twenty-four years."

A WARNING SYSTEM

Anger: that strange feeling, that puzzling response. It's a strong feeling of irritation. It's a signal—a warning system—telling you that something more is going on in your life than you're paying attention to. It's not a signal to be ignored either, like a postcard sent at a bulk rate. It's more like a special delivery letter telling you that you're being hurt, your rights are being trampled, you're living in fear, you're frustrated, or you're ignoring something significant in your life.

In many families the relationship between mother and daughter has the potential to be volatile and angry. It's a relationship in which deep feelings of care and love can exist along with intense anger. I've heard grown daughters say, "Oh, I love my mother. She's the best." And yet in the next breath they blame her for what's wrong in their lives. Have you ever felt like making these statements?

"She has never really understood me."

"She has never approved of any man I've dated."

"No matter what subject we talk about, she still tries to run my life."

"I wish she had paid more attention to me."

"I wish she had paid less attention to me."

"I wish she hadn't pushed me so hard."

"I wish she had pushed me more."

Daughters are possessive of their mothers and yet angry at them at the same time. Mothers and daughters can have a wonderful fulfilling relationship one day and be at painful odds the next. It's difficult to have such conflicting feelings. Victoria Secunda writes,

> No relationship is as highly charged as that between mother and daughter, or as riddled with expectations that could, like a land mine, detonate with a single misstep, a solitary stray word that, without warning, wounds or enrages. And no relationship is as bursting with possibilities of goodwill and understanding.[1]

There are as many reasons for angry feelings as there are

mother-daughter relationships. You could be feeling anger because you're trying too hard to please Mom but neglecting yourself; or maybe you're being doted on too much by others and feeling deprived of the chance to grow and become more independent.

In our survey, we asked women, "What angers you the most about your mother?" Here are some of their responses:

She wasn't there for me when I was growing up and now she wants me to be there for her since she's getting older.

Mother always wanted me slim and trim. The expression "fat chance" really applies here. Weight, my weight, has always been a problem for her. And it wasn't just her remarks about weight. It was all others. "People won't like you—you'll never get a husband, you won't fit in chairs."

I left the church. No, I left *her* church. It was the best thing I could have done. But she spread all these stories about me, saying I was on the fast track to hell. Is it possible to sue your own mother for slander?

She shouldn't have stayed with Dad and defended him so much. She never believed me when I told her about the abuse. It was all in my mind, she said. She should have helped me.

Her expectations made me feel like a failure. Most men couldn't do what she does. And is she ever opinionated! I've stopped mentioning much of anything since she knows so much. I don't need constant correction.

I'm angry because I can't really help her. We didn't have much of a relationship when I was young. Now that I've got my life together better I want to be close. But now she has Alzheimer's. I missed out as a child and now I'm missing out as an adult.

My mom died suddenly. I'm both angry and sad. She was too young. But I'm more upset over her life than her death. She had a rough time, and because of that I missed out too.

What about you? If your Mom angers you, why?

_____

_____

Do you express that anger? How?

_____

_____

Angry Expressions

We asked more than twenty-four-hundred women how they express their anger:

I'm a yeller when I get angry, so you better watch your step around me, because I'll let you know in no uncertain terms that I'm angry. It could be my husband, my daughter, or the dog that's going to hear me. I guess I want others to know that I'm angry. It's only fair to warn them. We had no warning in my home when I was younger. We were always ambushed by Mom or Dad. Maybe anger isn't always the best, but when it's there and I have to feel it, you're going to feel it as well.

When I get angry, I start crying. I don't know why. My husband tells me he would rather that I threw things or yelled, because he can't figure out whether I'm angry or hurt. You know, sometimes it's hard for me to decide which it is too.

Here is what happens to others when they get angry:

• I usually keep my anger inside and let it build until I'm basically fed up.

- I don't immediately express it. I rationalize the situation or I contemplate the cause and validity of my reaction to the cause.
- I get sarcastic and biting in my comments. I fish for someone to ask me what is wrong.
- I find it easy to stuff it and get depressed.
- I fume inside and get short with people. I do use words to express it, but I become snappy and impatient.
- I drive myself crazy.
- I get ugly. If I happen to walk by a mirror, I am surprised at how hateful I look. I want to hurt back with words. I want that person to be sorry they hurt me, and then I am sorry about my own selfishness.
- I am probably more negative. I tend to clam up, and I know that is wrong.
- I scream.
- I yell, then cry.
- I feel sad for feeling that way—then I lose my patience.
- I feel out of control and lash out—I regret my behavior later. I even hate myself at the time, but I can't seem to stop.
- I either button up for a while or I fly into a rage like a crazy person. *Sometimes* I can express myself passionately but in a controlled way.
- I hit a wall, throw something, yell, say something I regret, slam a door.
- I tend to yell and want to hit someone.
- I tend to draw inward with my emotions and then feel very guilty.
- I sometimes walk away and let it simmer underneath. Sometimes I raise my voice and express it. Sometimes I yell. Sometimes I take the person aside and talk calmly about it.

So why do people respond to anger in different ways? Somewhere you learned *what* to do with anger. That somewhere was your family. As you progressed through infancy to preschool and up through adolescence, you filed information about anger into your memory bank. Your family passed on to you a legacy of anger expression. It may have been healthy—and then again, it may not have been. How did your mother model anger for you? Do you remember?

HOW DID YOUR MOTHER MODEL ANGER FOR YOU?

——☕——

A number of women have told me they were thankful their parents showed their anger openly. "It helped me accept my anger. Mom gave me a good example of what to do with that irritation." Other women have told me, "Mom didn't ever tell me not to be angry but instead guided me to express it in healthy ways, which I appreciate." But many others don't appreciate what they saw and heard about anger. They either saw anger out of control or lived in a repressed, avoidant type of atmosphere. Some family members screamed and raged while others sulked or played the martyr role. Whatever pattern was there, it influenced you.

In our national survey, we asked the question, "As a child, the way I saw anger expressed was . . ." Here is a sampling of the results:

- Raised voices, foot stomping, clapping of hands together (Mom), silence (Dad).
- I usually wasn't allowed to show anger.
- Quiet steaming up.
- Loud voices, door slamming.
- "Mean" talking (rejection).
- My parents wouldn't speak to each other; my sister and I would argue.
- Yelling, tears.
- My mother would scream, hit cabinets, hit us with a brush on our bottoms; my siblings (the two older hated each other) and I tried to mediate.
- Loud voices; my father hit my mother; she became cold and distant.
- Physical abuse, verbal abuse; everyone always interrupting.
- Shaming and sarcastic expressions.

- Screaming; sometimes objects were thrown (Mother was volatile and explosive).
- My mom would say I never saw anger as a child because she was never angry; I think she's wrong.
- Voices were silenced; distance; sleep; work very hard; depression, illness (physical); tears; loud, fast talking, blaming, and then release.

Of all the unhealthy displays of anger in a home, the worst is *no display*—when anger is purposely avoided and not expressed. Many homes give the appearance of stability and healthy interaction. From all outward appearances the parents appear calm, consistent, and balanced. But anger still exists. You find it in the parents' tight lips, piercing looks, and painful and punishing silence that makes the children feel cut off from their love. Children don't dare to express their anger. It's forbidden. They're taught, "Not only do you not show your anger, you don't feel it either." As if that were possible!

Children in these families are taught a life-limiting pattern of denial. Perhaps you learned this pattern as a child. Or as an adult, you may be teaching your own child this behavior. But the denial of any emotion leads to an accumulation of it. Soon there's an overabundance, with no proper avenue for drainage. Denying an emotion means you have turned its energy back against yourself, and you're slowly destroying yourself and your potential.

Amanda, a well-put-together professional woman in her midthirties, was undergoing a very difficult experience. Her husband, Steve, was involved with another woman, and now Steve was leaving home. He had been telling Amanda a number of lies for some time, and it appeared that he planned to eventually divorce her.

"I want to know why I'm not angry at my husband for what he has done to me. I know that I should be angry. It would be normal. I was never angry as a child. Or I was never allowed to show those feelings. I was cooperative, but as I reflect back, I just can't really think of a time when I was ever angry. My mother ruled the home with a firm hand, and perhaps I learned it was best to smile and comply.

"Is that why I can't get angry now? Is there some connection between my upbringing and why I can't be angry at this time of my life?"

Amanda hit upon a good question and an "answer."

Some families can be described as anger-avoidant. In a family like this, either all or most of the members constantly work at minimizing their expressions of anger. Often the children carry this pattern with them and perpetuate it in their own families; if their spouses are the opposite, the pattern creates tremendous tension.

Once in a while a family like this actually allows one or more of its members to express their anger. Perhaps this family believes that fathers can get angry or that anger is a characteristic of a hyperactive child, a drinker, an overworked mother, and so on. But you can imagine how the angry persons are treated when they cut loose! Being ignored does very little to reduce one's anger.[2]

TAKE YOUR FAMILY'S HISTORY

You may feel as though you're the first person in your family to struggle with anger, but you're neither the first nor the last. If anger is a problem for you, it was a problem in previous generations as well. What you are struggling with is part of your family legacy that others also struggled with. That's why doing a family history on your family's emotions, especially anger, is so important. If you don't know about and understand your family's emotional history, you are more likely to repeat the patterns—regardless of their healthiness— or unconsciously react to them. If this is the case, you have not determined who you are or what you want for your own identity.

Reflect for a moment on your family and answer the following questions either from your own memories or by tapping into memories of other family members—siblings, aunts, uncles, or other significant and knowledgeable individuals. Try to determine what part their anger plays in your life at the present time:

When did your father get angry?
How did he express his anger?
Toward whom did he usually express it?

How long did it last?
What were the results at that time?
What is its effect upon you today?

When did your mother get angry?
How did she express her anger?
Toward whom did she usually express it?
How long did it last?
What were the results?
What is its effect upon you today?

When did a sibling get angry?
How did he or she express anger?
Toward whom did he or she usually express it?
How long did it last?
What were the results at that time?
What is its effect upon you today?

Jean's Story: The "Designated" Angry Person

Jean gave a fascinating account of anger in her family that is all too common.

You've heard of people being appointed an ambassador to a foreign country and representing their own country? Well, I received an appointment to represent my family, but it wasn't a pleasant one. I was appointed as the "angry family member." I was constantly told I was the angry one in the family—even when I wasn't! In time I just figured if that's what they wanted me to be, I'd go along with it. But over the years I discovered that I was the only one who expressed anger. At times I got the feeling they were waiting for me to get angry so they would feel better. They would provoke me until I got angry. I finally figured out they were releasing their own anger through me! I'd become the designated anger bearer! I wish they'd let their own anger out and quit using me!

Michelle's Story: The Great Pretender

Michelle came from a repressed home, at least in terms of anger. Even a voice raised in enthusiasm or intensity was considered anger. Both verbal and nonverbal expressions were given the label of anger.

I became the great pretender. I should have gone into theater work. I wore this pleasant mask that fooled everyone—except my body. Stuffing all the anger over the years and learning to smile instead made me feel like a fractured personality. In time my body rebelled. I can't stuff much of anything any more, since I lost half of my stomach. I guess my stomach kept score of all the hurts and frustrations. I don't like to smile much anymore either. It reminds me too much of living a lie; I wish my parents knew the result of their repression.

Teri's Story: The Bulldozer

Teri actually looked fierce when I met her. I don't usually say that about people, but there is no other way to describe her expression. It was fierce. Then I discovered why. Teri began by surprising me: "After we've talked for five minutes, Norm, you'll know all about my mother. And I won't be telling you one statement about her. I'm going to talk about me and from that and the way I respond, you'll see her. She's the biggest pain in my life, her and her anger. And guess who's the spitting image of her? I'm her replica!"

Teri was right! In no time at all her intensity deepened and her anger became apparent. I discovered that not only did her mother rage and run over others like a bulldozer leveling a building—so did Teri. The anger modeled at home found a seed in Teri, and it grew and flourished. Part of the reason was self-preservation. But what Teri learned crippled her relationships. It seemed that other people were following the advice of Proverbs 22:24–25: "Make no friendships with a man given to anger, and with a wrathful man do not associate, lest you learn his ways and get yourself into a snare" (AMP).

Kathy's Story: The Daughter Who Can't Break Free

Anger between a grown daughter and her mother often originates from the mother's over-involvement and inability to let go of her daughter.

Kathy was thirty and single, living on her own but still struggling with her mother's attempts to run her life. Though her mother lived on the opposite coast, Kathy told me that the three thousand miles between them hadn't helped to keep things calm. Her mother called once a week, tried to find out all the details of her daughter's life, and then proceeded to make a value judgment for each one.

"I know some of my standards are different than hers," Kathy said. "I've told her straight out about them and that nothing she says is going to change my mind. But it's like she doesn't even hear me. She's got to try to rule my life. Christmas is coming up and this year I've decided not to go home for a visit. I'm going to ski with some friends, and it's free. I can't really afford to fly to the East Coast. But I know if I said that, she would send a ticket and I would pay for going the rest of my life. I wish it could be different, but we just don't get along."

ANGER MANAGEMENT

Unfortunately, some moms can't be pleased. No matter what's done, it's never right. They have the ability to toss out verbal hand grenades, and when the grenades explode, Mom is the only one unscathed. Some mothers smother and others avenge. Some mothers have no ability to connect with their own daughters, and they end up deserting the child in some way. They never link up emotionally. If any of these mother types were part of your heritage, there is probably a pool of accumulated anger.[3]

YOUR ANGER TOWARD YOUR MOTHER COULD BE BASED ON YOUR NEED FOR HER APPROVAL.

The anger you feel toward your mother may exist because of unfilled expectations for her that you carry, or because of the cultural idealization we have that mothers are and need to be perfect.

Your anger toward your mother could be based on your need for her approval. When it isn't forthcoming or isn't as much as you want, anger protects you—but it also causes you to feel worse about yourself.

In *Don't Blame Mother,* Paula Caplan says:

> Energy spent in angry blaming of our mothers (and ourselves as both daughters and mothers) blocks our growth. One of the world's biggest sources of misdirected emotional energy is tied up in millions of women's rage at their mothers. Major works of art could be created, problems solved and identity crises resolved if the force in this obsessive mother-blaming were more productively channeled.[4]

Perhaps part of the purpose of any anger you feel toward your mother is to protect you or help you overcome your feelings of powerlessness. Often anger is a cry of "I don't want this situation to continue. I want it to be different."

But as you might have experienced, anger is one step that must lead to another, because it doesn't usually change another person, nor does it prevent a repeat of what you didn't like. Anger increases the distance between two people. It's imperative that you move beyond the anger you feel toward your mother, because anger often leads to women feeling guilty (more than men ever do). When guilt settles in, it generates still more anger toward Mother, since she's the reason for your guilt in the first place (or so you think).

I find that many women put themselves at the mercy of their mothers by basing their self-esteem and self-approval on them. This intensifies the daughters' needs for any morsels their mothers can give, and it reinforces their beliefs (true or false) that their mothers disapprove of them. All of this leads to anger, criticism of their mothers, and unfulfilling interactions with them—in short, a vicious cycle.

THE FEAR FACTOR

Do you have any fears about your mother? Since fear is one of the major contributors to anger, identifying a woman's mother-fears may help heal the problem so that it doesn't pass from generation to generation.

Mother-fears can be numerous, but three are significant: (1) the fear a woman has of losing her mother's love; (2) the fear a woman has of her mother dying; and (3) the fear of becoming like her mother and doing what she has done.

The fear you have of losing your mother's love is connected to the feeling you have that you can't please her or live up to her expectations. As you live with this fear, you are also afraid that she will die before you can please her. The frustration this fear incites can infuse still more anger into the relationship. The more you blame your mother for your problems, the greater your fear and suspicion that you are just like her.[5]

Caplan describes the process this way:

> If we regard our mothers as masochistic, rejecting, critical, demanding, guilt-inducing or just embarrassing, then we usually begin to suspect that we are, too. Most daughters try hard to avoid repeating what they consider the specific mistakes that their mothers made with them, and many daughters are determined to dress differently, to choose friends differently, to have different values from those their mothers have. At the same time, we often have an almost superstitious belief that we simply cannot avoid that repetition. We secretly fear that we are exactly like our mothers in all the ways that we dislike.
>
> Since we tend to believe that we are like our mothers, deprecation to them usually leads us also to self-deprecation. Hatred not only hurts the person who is hated; it is also destructive to the person who hates. Ultimately, hatred and blame keep us tied to the target of those feelings. They lead to our preoccupation with the target, who is always on our minds.[6]

Numerous women struggling with a mixture of feelings toward their mothers end up feeling sad because their own mothers will never match the image they have for them and because of the emotional distance that separates them from their mothers. When anger and sadness become too intense, emotional numbness and even alienation can set in. You create a wall to keep your mother out, but it keeps you locked up too. That wall also locks in your love. If your anger is not resolved, it may find its release in hostility toward a friend, your husband, or your own children, and thus the legacy is continued.

Are you angry with your mother? Take heart: some resolution is possible. You can learn to lower your expectations for your mother, identify her strengths, accept her faults (and even give her permission to have them), and disconnect your excessive need for her approval. All of this will lessen your anger.

We'll be discussing what to do with anger more thoroughly in the next chapter, but for now one of the first steps is to figure out if what you feel is really anger or something else.

ANGER'S PRECURSORS

Anger may be the first emotion we are aware of, but it is rarely the first emotion we experience in a particular situation. Where there is anger, there is almost always some kind of pain. Where there is pain, something is usually broken and needs to be fixed.

We've already talked about one of the emotions that most frequently precedes anger: *fear*. But *hurt* and *frustration* can also lead to anger. Not only are these emotions painful, but they also drain us of energy and increase our sense of vulnerability.

Hurt is one of those emotions we all experience but don't like to talk about. In fact, discussing hurt often means reliving the experience. When we're hurt we are vulnerable, weak, drained, hopeless, and helpless. If we try to deny or stuff our hurt into the unconscious, we may not think about it, but that doesn't mean it has magically disappeared. *Out of mind* does not mean *out of memory*. Over time it's easy for hurt to turn into boiling resentment.

Anger puts up a wall to protect us from hurt. The short-term effect is that we don't hurt. The long-term effect is that the problems we have been avoiding and trying to run from get worse and the hurt is always greater than it would have been if we had used our anger-energy to address the problem in the first place.

Eventually the layers of hurt, confusion, and misunderstanding make it more difficult to access the facts and interpretations that caused it. Unfortunately the pain of repressed hurt can simmer for years. Like smoke rising out of the campfire, anger can rise up out of the embers of hurt. If not dealt with, it can suddenly boil to the surface, moving past the potentially positive emotion of anger to the damaging emotion of rage.

Hurt is emotionally draining, and anger can give us the energy required to throw up walls to protect ourselves. At first the walls can keep people out and thus keep the hurt out. Anger can veil the hurt, fear, pain, and sense of loss that comes from real or perceived rejection. *If no one gets close to me, then no one can hurt me,* we think.

Many people are surprised to learn that hurt and anger go hand in hand. It's not uncommon to assume that the angry person is so insensitive they must be incapable of being hurt. That's just the point. Frequently the obnoxious person is the one who has experienced deep hurt, often in their childhood. It's a fact that we are more likely to feel anger toward people who are important to us.

Frustration is a normal response. It happens when others don't respond the way we want or expect. When an expectation isn't met, we become irritated. And that's what anger is—a strong feeling of irritation. One definition of *anger* is: "a deep chronic sense or state of insecurity and dissatisfaction arising from unresolved problems."

Much of a daughter's anger may be tied to frustration. To help sort through your feelings, list how or when your mom frustrates you:

1. What frustrates me about Mom is: _____

2. What frustrates me about Mom is: _____

3. What frustrates me about Mom is: _____

4. What frustrates me about Mom is: _____

5. What frustrates me about Mom is: _____

Which of these situations turns into anger?

Does frustration have to lead to anger? No. A little self-talk like the following can help: "I wish Mom [did so-and-so . . . or didn't . . . or wasn't . . .], but it's not the end of the world. She's been this way for years, so why should I be surprised? I can learn to think differently about what she says and does and learn new ways of responding."

WHAT DOES ANGER ACCOMPLISH?

Anger closes off communication. I've rarely met an angry person who is able to talk about what pains her when angry. Yet if you're unable to talk about what's hurting you when you're angry, how can others know what's bothering you? How can your mother change her response if you don't let her know how you felt wounded by what she said or did?

Anger keeps us feeling like victims. You feel helpless in spite of the strength of your anger because your anger doesn't let you fix what's wrong. When you blame or defend, your energy is diverted from resolving the original problem.

All of this is not to say that you should never become angry. Quite the contrary. It's when anger becomes your main line of defense that it becomes a difficulty. Every concern and issue has a solution, but anger doesn't usually lead you to that solution.[7]

So what can be done? Are there answers? Yes. The next chapter will give you some solutions.[8]

Chapter Six

GETTING OVER THE ANGER

So where do you go from here with your mother? You may have discovered you do experience fear, hurt, and frustration. Anger may or may not be involved. But please read on to learn about some new possibilities for resolving painful emotions that get in the way of peace. (Chapter 9 builds on this information by covering other aspects needed to heal a difficult mother-daughter relationship.)

To begin with, don't feel the need to apologize. If anger's there, accept it. It's yours. Use it for change. See it as a messenger telling you that something needs to improve. Then, with God's love and help, tackle the cause.

You can attempt to handle your anger with your mom in one of three ways. First, you can angrily confront her, tell her how she's wrong, and try to change her. This is futile.

A second way is for you to establish physical and emotional distance from Mom; the greater the distance, seemingly the better. This can bring some momentary relief but no resolution. The problem still exists and is activated anytime you visit her. Sometimes the anger is even redirected and expressed in a new relationship, such as with a spouse or close friend.

The best alternative is to learn a different, healthy response to your fears, hurts, or frustrations. Assert your own position constructively, regardless of what your mother does or how she responds. This is the one lasting solution.

There is a difference between expressing your anger aggressively and expressing it assertively. You can learn when you are using anger to defend and when you are using it to blame. Once you are able to

STOP BLAMING OTHER PEOPLE AND CONSIDER YOUR OWN RESPONSIBILITIES FOR CHANGE

express your anger without yelling, blaming, or attacking, you will feel better about what you are saying, and others will hear you more clearly.

When you express hurt and frustration in honest, controlled, and constructive ways, other people will be freed to be just as honest with you. This means exposing yourself to criticism and challenges from others. But this is good. Growth in your relationships can occur. It will force you to stop blaming other people and consider your own responsibilities for change. Constructive expression opens you up to an evaluation of your own behavior. The opposite approach for dealing with anger—suppression and being on the defensive—is ineffective.

CHOOSE YOUR RESPONSE

Start by turning your focus toward what you want out of feelings in your life, especially anger. Sounds strange, doesn't it, to rationally decide what to do with anger? This can involve viewing your mother in a different way, thinking about what type of relationship you want rather than focusing on what it is now, and rehearsing and practicing new responses instead of mulling over past scenarios again and again. It's possible to become independent without having to be emotionally distant.[1]

Learning to express what you think, believe, feel, and desire in a non-blaming, unapologetic way can bring results in any relationship and will reduce your own anger. But it takes effort, learning new approaches and ways of responding, practice, prayer, and the support of others to help you in this endeavor.[2]

Think about these questions for a moment:

• How do you want to express your anger in a constructive way?
• How do you want to respond to your mom's anger?

By answering these questions, you establish a goal and become a future thinker. That's positive. You are developing and drawing toward a vision for your life. When that happens, something dramatic will take place in your mind; you will begin to think the impossible is possible. Now, what can you do about anger?

Step 1: Accept it. We've mentioned it before, how important it is to break out of a repressive mode. Anger has a message for you, and it isn't to be denied. It's there for a reason: to point out the need to resolve the cause.

Step 2: Commit your situation to the Lord. Time and time again we have seen God meet people's deepest needs and bring peace to relationships. Ask Him to give you clarity of thought, wisdom, and patience. In Proverbs 16:32 we read, "He who is slow to anger is better than the mighty" (NASB). Why? Because being "hasty in spirit" is similar to experiencing "vexation of spirit." And to grow vexed or to become agitated in times of distress only makes matters worse.[3]

Step 3: Discover the reason for your anger. What is the *real* cause in each situation? As you look at each situation or encounter in which you are angry, ask yourself, "What's really bothering me, and what would I like to change?" Then ask, "What can I do to bring about change?"

WHAT IS THE HEALTHIEST WAY TO RESPOND?

There are three kinds of situations in life: (1) situations you can control or change; (2) situations you can influence; and (3) situations you can do nothing about.

Don't increase your frustration (and thus your anger) by trying to change situations you can do nothing about. If the cause of your anger falls under this category, your only choice is to continue to give it to the Lord in prayer and turn your attention to things you can change or influence.

If it is a situation you *can* change or influence, get out a sheet of paper for the next step.

Step 4: Make a list of your options. Don't worry about how practical your ideas are; just fill the sheet with as many constructive alternatives as you can think of. This may go slowly at first, but once you get the hang of it you may be surprised at how creative you can be.

A lot depends on what you want for your life and in your relationship with your mom. Would you like to be at a place where you can forgive her? Be reunited? Reconciled? Free from bitterness?

Some daughters aren't sure.

Some daughters simply don't want things to change. Now, the very fact that you are reading this book indicates you'd like your relationship with your mom to change; you'd like peace. But we want you to consider deep down what may seem like a strange question: Are you getting anything out of being estranged from your mother? Are there benefits for you? This isn't a judgmental question or one that implies you shouldn't be where you are in your relationship. But even in a painful situation there may be rewards such as freedom from the pain of Mom's remarks or questions. Perhaps you receive compassion from others, sympathy, protection, safety, and so on. List any positives you see for not being at peace with your mom:

_____

_____

_____

These beneficial "side effects" could be why you might prefer to stay where you are in the relationship. But let's look at the other side, what we call the price tag. What's this costing you? What price would you pay by not attempting to heal your relationship?

_____

_____

_____

If you've decided that a response is appropriate, determine the most favorable time and manner in which you can communicate it. A good rule of thumb is to deal with a problem as soon as you become aware of it and have had time to choose how you can best express your feelings. Anger can vary in its intensity. If you are experiencing mild anger, you can usually deal with the situation on the spot. However, if your anger is moderate to strong, it is usually wise to wait until you've taken time to think and pray it through.

It is always better to express your anger at the source of your hurt. Yes, you might be angry at your mom, but what's the specific reason? If you've bought into the myth that revealing angry feelings only destroys relationships, this may be difficult for you to do. But the only way to pull the teeth out of that lion of fear is to do it. Challenge the misbelief. Risk speaking the truth in love.

EXPRESS YOUR ANGER AT THE SOURCE OF YOUR HURT

One thirty-year-old daughter thought it best to address her frustrations with her mom—and ideas for change—in a letter:

Mom. I have a few suggestions to make, which I feel could make our relationship run smoother. I'd appreciate your considering these and thinking about their possibilities of helping both of us.

Sometimes I feel besieged by questions and feel interrogated. If there is something going on that I feel you need to know or would be interested in, I will let you know. Or if you have a concern, just say, "Could you give me some more information about . . ." and I'll respond. Some subjects I want to discuss with you and some I may not at a particular time.

I am different from you, and my generation is also different. I know that is sometimes difficult to handle. But there are positives in differences. Even though I don't take all your suggestions, I hear you and do consider them. I like it when you ask if I want some advice, but I need to have the freedom to say "yes," "no," or "I'll consider it."

Here is an agreement a daughter and mother made:

- We will respect each other's point of view and not assume we know what the other is thinking or feeling.
- We will respect each other's feelings; we will tell the truth, but we will be tactful.
- We will respect the value of our relationship by keeping this agreement private. Neither of us will discuss it with anyone else, either friend or family.[4]

Our next suggestion is something you might not expect.

Step 5: Write a prayer—a visionary prayer—in the form of a letter. Write a letter to God telling Him about the next years of your life and how, with His strength and guidance, anger will have a different place in your life. Take the time to do this. Read this letter out loud, not just once but each week.

Step 6: Choose forgiveness. The best definition of forgiveness is "wishing the other person well." It involves letting go. It is like holding a pen tightly in your hand, then opening your hand and watching the pen drop to the floor. Remember playing tug-of-war as a child? As long as the parties on each end of the rope are tugging, you have a "war." But when someone lets go, the war is over. When you forgive your mother, you are letting go of your end of the rope. No matter how hard she may tug on the other end, if you have released your end, the war is over for you.

Breaking Free From Burdens

Here's another illustration. Imagine you're getting ready for a trip that you're really looking forward to. You bring out the soft-sided suitcase you just purchased because it can hold a lot. You begin to select the items you want to take with you. The piles seem to grow, but you should be able to fit everything in. Your suitcase begins to bulge and expand, but that's what it's supposed to do. Finally you get everything in and sit on it so you can close the zipper. It doesn't have the same shape it used to, but that's all right. You try to lift it, but it barely budges. The only way to get it to your car and then the destination is to drag it. Already you're beginning to wonder if you need all this stuff and if it's worth the hassle. The trip is beginning to feel like a burden rather than a pleasure.

This is the way it is for many daughters who've been hurt by their mother. They wake up in the morning, fill a huge suitcase with all memories and hurts, and then pack the real stuff—anger, injustices, resentment. Some daughters have a mixture of feelings and memories—not only for what they missed out on but what they will never have. They also itemize how Mom failed them and add to it how they've failed themselves. It's just baggage, but it's excess baggage. And it's not like you can ship this suitcase on ahead of you. It's handcuffed to you so you drag it everywhere—it weighs you down, drains your energy, and hinders your progress. Worse yet, the suitcase contains things you don't even need.[5] You're carrying a grudge.

Grudge. It's not a nice-sounding word, is it? It sits in your throat like a lump. A grudge comes when you've collected injustices that feed anger. It's like an emotional scab that's been picked at for so long it's now infected, and the poison begins to move into every area of your life. How do you know if you're carrying a grudge? There's an energy drain. It's used on remembering hurts and keeping score. It's used on rehearsing what you would like to

THE POISON BEGINS TO MOVE INTO EVERY AREA OF YOUR LIFE

say and thinking of ways to punish the other person. It's letting anger fester even to the point of rage. You look for ways to initiate payback. Another way to determine if grudges exist is to look at your physical and emotional health. There are physical fallouts to grudges—stress, elevated blood pressure, ulcers, colitis, arthritis, etc.

There's also emotional fallout since we project onto others the issues we've had with Mom. Suspicion, hypersensitivity, and negativity are a few of the results. Grudges hurt the person holding them. They're not worth it. They're unbiblical. They will only get you what you don't want in life.[6]

One of my favorite authors on the subject of forgiveness is Lewis Smedes. Think about your mom as you read this:

> Forgiving is the only way to heal the wounds of a past we cannot change and cannot forget. Forgiving changes a bitter memory into a grateful memory, a cowardly memory into a courageous memory, an enslaved memory into a free memory, and more than anything else forgiveness gives birth to hope for the future after our past illusions have been shattered.[7]

I've heard many say, "I could forgive my mom if only she would own up to what she did and apologize."

As you think about forgiveness, what are three things you wish your mother would apologize for?

1. _____

2. _____

3. _____

What will it do for you if she apologizes?

_____

_____

What will it do for you if she doesn't apologize?

_____

_____

Can you think of three things you need to apologize to your mom for?

1. _____

2. _____

3. _____

If you were to apologize, what would you like to hear in response?

_____

_____

Is there anything else you would like your mother to do that would enable you to forgive her?

_____

_____

Yes, forgiving your mother may be difficult. But forgiveness is the one way to move ahead in life and experience God's abundance and grace. It's the ultimate step to healing a wound. You may not feel ready yet. You may not think Mom deserves forgiveness. But this is what forgiveness is all about. *None of us deserves forgiveness.* It's got to be a gift. It's a gift that will give you freedom.

One way to initialize your act of forgiveness is to write a statement of release. Here are some models that you can use for your own personal situation with your mother:

Mom, I release you from determining how I feel and how I respond to others in my life. I release you from the anger and resentment that I have held toward you and others in my life because of you. This includes anger and resentment for . . .

I no longer hold you responsible for my happiness. I release you from my expectations of who you should have been, what you should have done, and . . .

Mom, I release you for not being there for me emotionally and for your silence over the years. I don't know why you weren't there. I don't need to know.

Mom, I was mad at you for dying when I was a child and not giving me a chance to get to know you. I missed out on so much. I blamed you. I'm sorry. I hope you're in heaven.

I forgive you.

Forgiveness, especially for years of neglect, abandonment, or control, doesn't come easy. If you find yourself struggling to express positive feelings toward your mother, unresolved resentment may be hiding within you. There is a way to uncover those feelings and clear the way for moving ahead.

Take a blank sheet of paper and at the top write, "Dear Mom." Under the salutation, write the words "I forgive you for . . ." Then complete the sentence by stating something your mother did that has bothered you all these years. For example, "I forgive you for not affirming me."

What is the first thought you had after writing that sentence? It may be a rebuttal to the forgiveness you're trying to express. It may be an emotional protest against what you've written. For example, the woman who is forgiving her mother for not affirming her may remember how her mother made fun of her outfit one particular Sunday or belittled an accomplishment.

Whatever your thought might be, write another "I forgive you for . . ." statement for it. Keep writing "I forgive you for . . ." statements for every thought that comes to the surface. Don't be discouraged if your angry protests contradict the desire to learn to forgive, or if they're so strong that it seems like you have not expressed any forgiveness at all. Remember, you're in the *process* of forgiving your mother; continue to write until all the pockets of resentment and resistance have been drained.

Some complete this exercise with only a few statements. Others have more resentment to clear away, and they continue writing for several pages. You will know you have completed your work when you write "I forgive you for . . ." and can't think of any more responses to complete the statement.

After you have finished writing, sit facing an empty chair and read your statements of forgiveness aloud. Imagine your mother sitting there accepting your forgiveness with both verbal and nonverbal affirmation. Take as long as you need for this process, explaining and amplifying your statements as you go, if necessary. I sat and listened to such a reading in my office for fifteen minutes one day.

Don't show this list to anyone; it's unnecessary. When you're finished verbalizing your statements, destroy the entire list. Burn it or tear it into little pieces symbolizing that "the old has gone, the new has come!" (2 Corinthians 5:17).

SEEING REALISTICALLY

As we wind down our suggestions for relieving anger, the next idea may be another unexpected one.

Step 7: You may need to forgive yourself. But why? There are several reasons. You may be blaming yourself and feeling guilty for:

- not being able to change—or cure—your mother's problem;
- not living up to her expectations for you no matter how unreasonable;
- not being loved and accepted by her because of a defect in your appearance or personality;
- not being perfect in some way or every way;
- treating yourself the way your mother treated you;
- mistreating yourself when you have difficult times (as a result of your past);
- developing some of the same tendencies or problems you despise in your mother.

Isn't it ironic that we often take out our frustrations on ourselves rather than on the people who hurt us? Perhaps we consider ourselves a safer target than the offenders. If your mother has hurt you, you may feel that you can't vent your frustration on her because she'll only hurt you again. So you take the path of least resistance by shouldering the blame. This isn't necessary. It wasn't before and it isn't now.[8]

At some point you need to accept the reality of who your mother was and is. Parents don't always know what they are doing or know what is right and wrong. Perhaps your mom did the "right" thing most of the time, but perhaps not. Your mother may have had her own difficult background and personal deficits, and these have probably impacted you. Without excusing her behavior, you need to let go of these negative experiences. It's the only method of ending the war between the two of you and gaining control. Otherwise, you're letting what happened control you.

Forgiveness is a medicine for pain. It heals the pain of a wounded memory and the hole in a heart. It relieves seething rage, resentment, and the choke hold of hate.

Forgiveness happens within you. It's completed in your head and mind. It means you see your mother as worthy of your love. And for many of you, forgiving yourself and forgiving your mother are vital steps that will lead to a healthier relationship. For others, though, the relationship won't be any closer because Mom will make no effort to change.

Nancy asked, "If I forgive my mother, does that mean I have to spend time with her? I don't want to be bitter, but she hasn't changed. She hasn't acknowledged what she's done. I don't want a reunion." There is a difference between forgiveness and a reunion. Lewis Smedes described it:

It takes one person to forgive.
It takes two to be reunited.
Forgiving happens inside the wounded person.
Reunion happens in a relationship between people.
We can forgive a person who never says [she] is sorry.
We cannot be truly reunited unless [she] is honestly sorry.
We can forgive even if we do not trust the person who
    wronged us once not to wrong us again.
Reunion can happen only if we can trust the person who
    wronged us once not to wrong us again.
Forgiving has no strings attached.
Reunion has several strings attached.[9]

If a changed relationship and reunion with your mother seems impossible, don't give up hope.

Step 8: Release your past and your mother to the Lord. Pray for her, perhaps in a new way. Pray about her weaknesses, pray for her growth, and ask God's blessing upon her life. Pray for a new relationship with your mom. Pray for the Lord's renewing strength. Ask Him to show you how He sees you, and use that knowledge to see your mother in the same way—worthy, valued, and a "new creation."[10]

Chapter Seven

MOM WASN'T THERE

Loss. It's a simple four-letter word used when something is lacking in a person's life. There's a hole where there should be substance, and it produces everything from an ache or a longing to depression. In a mother-daughter relationship, we usually think of loss as the absence of the mother. She has died or left the family, so she's not part of her daughter's life. But most of the time, mother-daughter losses exist when they're in each other's lives. If a daughter doesn't have her mom's approval, that's a loss. If the relationship is distant, that too brings a loss. If a daughter sacrifices her dreams, her way of responding to life, or her career in order to satisfy her mother or gain approval, that is a loss. If a daughter defers to her mother's wishes, she gives up control or power, and that too is a loss. If a mother is stingy with affirmations, the daughter lived with loss. If her mother was a substance abuser, there were losses.

Loss associated with your mother hurts—no matter how or when it happens.

Mom was there but not there, if that makes any sense at all. She was around the house but not involved in my life. I felt like I was getting leftovers from the table, if I got anything at all. We weren't connected, not like my girl friends were with their mothers. Mom wasn't dead, but in many ways our relationship was.

I grew up feeling odd, as though there were some defect in me. My mom left my dad when I was five, but she left her children as well. I can understand divorcing your spouse, but not divorcing your children. There were three of us, and Mom saw us maybe once a month, and it wasn't for long either. I always wondered as a child what was wrong with me, but now I wonder what was wrong with her. I guess I blame her for every problem I've had and I'm angry.

An Identity Crisis

Loss of a mother can include several types of absence, such as premature death, mental illness, physical separation, dementia, neglect, or abandonment. If a grown daughter loses her mother, as painful as it might be, the daughter's identity and personality is already formed and fairly intact and she has greater resources with which to handle the loss and ensuing grief. But if the loss happens during childhood or adolescence, the loss becomes part of her identity and can affect how she develops and responds to the world, especially if the loss is the result of the mother's sudden death. A girl who loses her mother is forced to grow up cognitively and behaviorally faster than her friends. She might grow up feeling the world owes her because she lost her mother too soon. Some adult responsibilities may be passed on to her, all without the support from her mother and an intact family. If there is no other mother-type figure in her life, it's more difficult to develop and build her feminine self-image. Some daughters find themselves feeling as though a part of them is "stuck" in their childhood or adolescence. In many ways a daughter is on her own, moving forward by herself.[1]

One of the most difficult mother absences is when she is physically near but emotionally distant and unavailable. We hear much about the Phantom Father today (see my book *Always Daddy's Girl*), but the description applies just as much to mothers who are absent and detached. Mom doesn't provide what is needed in order to connect with her. She fails to properly nurture her daughter or provide the safety and sense of belonging that is needed. If your mother didn't invest in you emotionally, you probably didn't invest in her either. How might the Phantom Mother's legacy show up? The home is a child's training ground for future relationships, so if a daughter doesn't learn to relate to her mother, it's no wonder that other relational difficulties occur. The daughter could experience shallowness in relationships, aloofness, withdrawal, mistrust, anger, or aggression and expect others to fulfill what her mother didn't.[2] The fortunate daughters are the ones who find surrogate mothers or substitutes who provide what Mother could not or did not provide.

IF YOUR MOTHER DIDN'T INVEST IN YOU EMOTIONALLY, YOU PROBABLY DIDN'T INVEST IN HER EITHER

LOOKING FOR CLOSURE

In some ways, when a mother divorces or abandons the family, it's worse than a death. In grief counseling we talk about the various kinds of losses and which are the most difficult to handle. Of all the losses experienced in relationships, *ambiguous* loss is the most devastating kind because it is unclear. There is no certainty or closure about a person's absence or presence.

There are two types of ambiguous loss. One is when a family member is physically absent but still there psychologically in the hearts and minds of the family members. They have no idea where the person is physically. Traditionally, this kind of absence has included runaway or kidnapped children, missing soldiers, or accidents in which the body can't be found. But this can also include absent mothers who have left because of divorce or some other reason. As her child left behind, you never hear from her and wonder, *Where is she?*

Abandonment leaves in its wake a confused daughter. *Mom is alive but unavailable. Mom is alive but didn't want me. Where is she? What did I do to cause her to leave?* You can imagine what this does to a daughter's self-esteem. And it's difficult to mourn the loss of a mother when she's not dead; most daughters don't want to give up hope

121

that Mom will return someday and all will be well![3]

Listen to the words of a daughter whose mother left her when she was two-and-a-half months old:

> Although I did not experience the death of my mother, in an odd way her absence could be viewed as a death. She was missing from the family picture, and no one wanted to talk about her. I suppose for all practical purposes, she was dead. I, too, have had to do some mourning for the loss of my dreams about her. I spent some time in therapy trying to put all of my behavior patterns into some kind of order. During one session we had a mock funeral for the "dream mother." I had no idea how difficult that mourning would be. I've survived, battered but intact. I still have a long way to go with putting all of the past behind me, but my prayer is that one day I can lead a full life and be the person that I want to be.[4]

The second type of ambiguous loss is when the person is physically present but psychologically absent. This includes those with addictions, strokes, mental illnesses, comas, or Alzheimer's disease. But this kind of loss could also be expanded to include those who neglect their families—mothers who are physically there but emotionally absent. In these cases there is often an endless search that goes on—maybe not a physical search, but one within the heart and mind. It feels like a loss, but it may not be recognized as such by others.

The daughter lives with the hope that someday things will be all right. The author of *Motherless Daughters* describes it like this: "The mother is physically present but offers no emotional substance, like the body of a car with nothing under the hood. But the daughter keeps turning the key in the ignition, hoping that if she does it just right, the motor might start up this time."[5]

The sense of loss is so evident when you listen to the many women who told us how their mothers weren't there for them.

Even though I told her how her third husband behaved toward me when she wasn't around, she did nothing about it. Finally, I had enough and blew up. She told me to get out of the house before she got home from work. It was her husband, she said, and her house, and she couldn't afford it without him. So with a broken heart, no money, and nowhere to go, I left.

Her physical absence left a huge void—the sense of security, stability, nurturing, hugs, etc. Part of my resentment and anger toward her over the years has been because she has missed so much. She has been present for many of the milestones in my life—birthdays, graduation, the big stuff—but she missed out on so much of the smaller, everyday stuff. There have been so many times that I have wanted to talk with her, ask her a question, or just have her feel like a mom to me, and I haven't been able to reach her, or even known where she was.

She rarely seemed to have time for me or my brothers and sister when we were growing up. Other people and their perception of her were much more important. She is a hoarder, which made our home practically unlivable. I could never have friends over to visit. She has frequently not been very loving and supportive of my dad, though he has always cared and provided for her and treated her with love and respect.

To be brutally honest, she was a lousy role model as a wife. She waged a cold war against my dad from the time I was a teenager until the day he was diagnosed with terminal cancer. For roughly thirty-two years I watched my mom "tear down her house with her own hands."

She was not a good spiritual role model. She rarely read her Bible. Her public prayers were awkward and full of

Christian phrases that she would string together without any particular rhyme, reason, or meaning. She attended good Bible-believing churches all her life, yet her talk never matched her walk.

She was sort of an adult child. Her mom died when she was twenty-six and she never got over that. Later my brother died in an accident and she really seemed to withdraw.

My mother wasn't demonstrative, verbally or physically. I don't remember many hugs. She seemed to pit siblings against each other. She had a hard time being a "mom" and did not protect me against my father.

She allowed my father, who was an alcoholic, adulterer, and abuser (physically and emotionally), to chase us out of our home in the middle of one night. He attempted to kill us too many times to count. She frequently told me I was crazy because I was not like her or the rest of the family.

She turned her back on me when I was four and told her my brother and sister raped me. She didn't believe me and allowed the sexual abuse to continue for twenty-three years. The memories aren't all clear but I believe she took me to the ER for a saline abortion when I was between the ages of nine and eleven. All she could say was "I'm sorry" over and over as I agonized in labor. My brother impregnated me and they had to destroy the evidence of incest.

For starters, she wasn't "there" for herself. And she never made me feel like a worthwhile, beautiful, unique, and cherished daughter. It was her job and she didn't do it!

She was emotionally absent. She was never able to say anything nice to me. She never went out of her way to make any special time together for us. My mother used to sarcastically tell my father that I was so wonderful, as if she was jealous that my dad loved me. I felt very alone, very confused, very sad, and my dad left me anyway.

She was in bed a lot, so I used to do a lot of cleaning, cooking, and other chores, including taking care of my older brother. I had to do things perfectly or my father would beat me with a belt. She refused to teach me, so I taught myself and made lots of mistakes.

There was no laughter in our house. Mom and Dad fought daily over every decision. We didn't have friends or relatives come to our house. We didn't play games, have fun, or go on vacations. Our house was messy and never decorated. She did not teach me to do the basics of life.

My mom was extremely promiscuous. All I can remember is having an endless procession of men going in and out of our house. Many nights I had to sit outside while she visited with them. She had an awful reputation and I have felt "guilty by association" my whole life. She made me feel dirty.

I never felt loved or wanted. In fact, she stated many years ago that she had never wanted children.

I was never taught to express myself verbally or think things through or make decisions. I was not prepared in any way to interact with others. My mother was incapable emotionally of having a relationship.

I always felt she was ashamed of me because I was in the lower reading group in elementary school, whereas my sister (seven years younger) was in the advanced reading group. I never felt that my opinion mattered. She never talked to me about my art or encouraged it.

When my mother drank, she would tell me to watch my younger brother and sister while she ran to the store. She would come back the next day with a hangover and bruises all over her body. Later I found out she was an alcoholic.

She did not communicate well. I learned all the basics of life from friends and a lot of trial-and-error. It seemed that she only showed me love and kindness when I was sick. So I was sick a lot. Emotionally she was all over the map, so the house did not feel stable.

She died when I was sixteen and just starting to date. I was full of questions.

Looking back, I feel her discipline could have been stronger in certain areas; she sometimes "looked the other way" on certain teenage issues instead of confronting my undesirable behavior.

She stayed married to an abusive man, my father, who dishonored her regularly. I married someone very similar to my dad because it felt comfortable, it felt like "home." Although my parents fought a lot, I still loved my home.

She didn't ever give me advice, direction, or counsel. I'm thirty-five now, and looking back I was so lost, made so many terrible decisions. Both of my parents worked full time, so I feel they were absent during my childhood.

There was never an emotional bonding between us. I knew she loved me, but we never had a close relationship with each other.

There were times when she would embarrass me in front of friends and relatives about my bad habits. She still has trouble "taming her tongue" today. She will often divulge secrets and shout out her strong opinions in mixed company, at times when it's better to keep quiet.

Because she lived by legalistic rules that tended to define who she was and how she was doing spiritually, I wasn't allowed to fail in some areas. I felt a tremendous pressure to be perfect, and never really embraced how I measured up in God's eyes until I was about thirty years old.

My relationship with my mom was tumultuous as I was growing up. Our personalities are very different—she has the stronger will and stronger personality, and used it to keep me in line. I mostly behaved because I preferred peace and because I wasn't clever or quick enough to ever win verbal battles with her.

I discovered that I couldn't trust her with personal information or be vulnerable about my struggles because she would either immediately "preach" at me without listening to me first, or she would use the information against me later.

I learned that mute obedience kept things smoother. Disagreement equaled disrespect and insubordination in my mother's eyes. By the things she said or how she handled situations, Mom inferred that God was always on her side. How can a kid trump that?

Mom held out perfection as the standard to which I measured. I got the message that if something wasn't perfect, then it was a complete failure, and I, by extension, was a failure as a human being. For a long time I tried very hard to live up to her expectations, but I eventually gave up.

THE AGING MOTHER

Until now, our discussion on losses has focused mostly on childhood experiences. But many daughters suffer additional loss later in the life, when their mother ages.

Growing older involves endings and beginnings; having to make changes and having changes made for us. Not only do you change, but your parents are changing too. And some of the changes in their life may trouble you.

YOU COULD VERY WELL BECOME YOUR MOTHER'S CAREGIVER

In later years a role reversal often occurs. The parent becomes the child and the child becomes the parent. You could very well become your mother's caregiver. One study indicated that the average daughter will spend approximately eighteen years taking care of her mother. As one woman said, "I spent eighteen years raising each of my children and thought I was all through with that part of my life. Now I'm having to parent an adult; my own mother!"[6]

This role reversal usually comes about gradually. Over a period of years you begin to realize that control has begun to shift from your parents to you. You find that responsibility is being transferred from their shoulders to yours, and now—despite everything that might have happened in the past—it's your duty to care for them.

You could hear yourself saying things like, "You're sick, Mom? Have you called the doctor? Of course, you have the number. He's been your physician for thirty-five years. All right, I'll call the office and tell them you're coming. You get ready and I'll be there to drive you over there."

Or, "Did you take your medicine today? I know it tastes bad, but it's good for you and the doctor says you have to take it."

Or, "Mom, you shouldn't walk down to the post office without your sweater. Don't you know it's cold this early in the morning?"

Or maybe you will hear your mom say, "All the kids used to come here for the big Christmas dinner. I kind of miss that. Whose house are we going to this year?"

You might find yourself taking the broom out of your mom's

hands because it's "too much work for her" or reconciling your mother's checkbook because "she never seems to get it right."

Then one day you'll be doing Mom's laundry, washing her hair, telling her what she should and shouldn't eat. You might get impatient as she dawdles around while you're waiting for her shopping.

As a forty-eight-year-old woman describes it, "It wasn't supposed to be like this. For years I was the one who was bathed, dressed, fed, consoled, taught, disciplined, ordered around, and cared for. I patiently waited for my turn to come when I could command and be independent. Now that it's here, why am I so sad?"

When we see our parents behaving in such a changed or dependent manner, we sometimes become angry and impatient with them. Perhaps it's because we cannot handle their increased limitations. Perhaps it reminds us that we will face the same changes as we age. We do not like what we see, but we can do nothing about it. Life is following its pattern.

At this time in life we perhaps have greater emotional control; we need to exercise it. Life is limited, making it all the more important to do what you can to find peace with your mother.

FACING THE PAST

To find healing today—and to set the stage for whatever the future holds—take a moment to think about your personal sense of loss with regard to your mother. The following questions may help.

- As you reflect upon your mother, in what way was she absent from your life?
- If your mother left physically, what was the reason for her leaving? Who was most influential in making that decision?
- How old were you at the time, and how did you learn of her leaving?
- Did you think you were the cause of her leaving?
- What are five effects upon your life because of your mother's absence?
- With whom did you discuss her going at the time?

We have to face the past to confront the present. It's not easy.

It can be painful. Many are reluctant to "face the unacceptable."

Dr. David Stoop has suggested several steps in this process.[7] Your *first step* is identifying the symptoms of this loss in your life. These are the places where it hurts. Here are several questions that can help you identify what happened and when.

My relationship with my mother in preschool was . . .

_____

_____

My best experience with her at that time was . . .

_____

_____

My worst experience with her at that time was . . .

_____

_____

My relationship with my mother in elementary school was . . .

_____

_____

My best experience with her at that time was . . .

_____

_____

My worst experience with her at that time was . . .

_____

_____

My relationship with my mother during adolescence was . . .

_____

_____

My best experience with her at that time was . . .

_____

_____

My worst experience with her at that time was . . .

_____

_____

Finding Your Real Mom

The *second step* in the healing process is to identify what is true about your mother and what isn't: what is factual, what has been reinterpreted, and what you don't know about her. Recovery could involve learning some things about your mother you would rather not know. As you enter this search-and-discovery phase of your journey, ask God to be your guide as well as an informant. Ask Him to lead you to both the truth and the information you need to know.

How do you go about this? First, identify what you would like to know about your mother—the questions you need answered. Then go to relatives and friends of your mother and simply ask your questions. Ask co-workers also, if any are available. Be aware that you will come up against contradictions as you go through this process. If your mother is available, interview her. Perhaps the use of photos can help you in this process. Sometimes all it takes is a question.

Sharing Your Feelings About the Past

The *third step* requires a trusted person with whom you can share. It's time to talk about your feelings about yourself, what you've learned, and how you feel about what you've learned. One of the best ways to begin is to *write out* how you feel (longhand rather than on a computer), because the "drainage process" can be very helpful. Sometimes it's best to talk first with a close friend, pastor, or counselor, and then eventually a trusted family member. You may discover you're not alone in your thoughts and feelings.

The *fourth step* is important as well: Re-create the past.

"Oh, if only it could have been different" is a comment I often hear. It's wistful thinking, but often followed with, "Oh well, no sense wasting time on that." But it's not a waste of time. It's helpful to dream about the way you think it should have been because it helps you identify all the things you lost. No one else will do this for you, so you're the one to step out and think about your past. You could do this in a number of ways. You could write the story the way you think it should have been, or you could complete a series of "I wish . . ." statements.

- "I wish my mother had . . ."
- "I wish my mother hadn't . . ."
- "I wish my mother had said . . ."
- "I wish my mother hadn't said . . ."
- "I wish my mother would say to me today . . ."
- "I wish my mother wouldn't say to me today . . ."

There can be a host of feelings underlying your losses. The best way to access the feelings you have is to look at your history and identify what you wish were true (which amounts to a loss), then look at the Ball of Grief illustration above and identify what you are feeling. If you're angry, write, "I'm angry because . . ." If you're fearful, write, "I'm fearful because . . ." You need to express it in writing—and then give it to God. Say to Him, "God, I'm giving you this. Take it and drain it from my life. I want to move on." Reading other books on loss, grief, anger, or worry can give you other practical steps to take.

Saying Good-bye

The *final step* is to actually grieve. Grief is not an orderly process. It can be disrupted. The following steps have helped many others with the grief process.[8]

1. Try to identify what doesn't make sense to you about the losses you experienced with your mother. It could be the "why" question, which is both a question and a cry of protest. Even if your mother could give you an answer, it probably wouldn't satisfy you. It's like our cry of "Why?" to God. If He ever answered us, we'd probably still argue with Him.

You may wonder, *Did my mom love others? Did she have any idea, any guilt over what she didn't do for me? When she didn't come to my concert, did she know how much that hurt me?*

2. Identify your emotions and feelings that were already thought about or written down. Since this is an ongoing process, do you see any change in their intensity over a period of a few days? Is there an increase or a decrease? Remember, if you're facing some of the new losses for the first time, feelings can be more intense than before.

3. Identify the steps you will take to move ahead and overcome these losses you suffered because of your mother. It is a helpful way to identify what you've done in the past as well.

4. Don't try to handle your losses by yourself. Share this journey with someone else, and remember your journey through grief will never be exactly like that of another person. Yours will be unique.

5. If you know of others who have experienced a similar loss and recovery, talk with them. Their story will have similarities and dissimilarities but could be helpful.

6. Identify the positive characteristics and strengths of your life that have helped you before. Which of these will help you at this time of your life?

7. When you pray, don't hold back any feelings. Share everything you are experiencing.

8. Think about where you want to be in your relationship with your mother a year from now. Describe this in as much detail as possible. Put it into a story or letter to yourself, or express it as a prayer to God.

9. Remember that understanding grief intellectually isn't sufficient. It can't replace the emotional experiences of living through this difficult time. You need to be patient and allow your feelings to catch up with your mind. Expect fluctuations in your feelings and remind yourself that these are normal.

10. One of the most important steps in recovery is being able to say *good-bye*. When you do this, you're acknowledging that you're no longer going to share your life with those hurts, unfulfilled dreams, or expectations. For some, saying good-bye is a one-time occurrence, while others need to do this on several occasions. One of the best ways of doing this is writing a good-bye letter(s) and then reading it aloud as you commit the contents to God.

When you're able to grieve, you are able to take care of unfinished issues in your life. Not addressing your losses keeps you cemented to the past. Saying good-bye is an important step in this process. Life is a series of hellos, good-byes, and hellos.

How do you feel when you say good-bye? Sad? A feeling of, "I wish it wasn't so," or a sense of relief? The word *good-bye* originally meant *God be with you* or *Go with God*, and it was a recognition that God was a significant part of the passage. It helps to know that as you grieve you will be strengthened when you remember that God is there in your journey with you.

Listen to the words from the writer of *Praying Our Good-byes:*

We all need to learn to say good-bye, acknowledge the pain that is there for us, so we can eventually move on to another hello. When we learn to say good-bye we truly learn how

to say to ourselves and to others: Go. God be with you. I
entrust you to God. The God of strength, courage, comfort,
hope, love is with you. The God who promises to wipe away
all tears will hold you close and will fill your emptiness. Let
go and be free to move on. Do not keep yourself from
another step in your homeward journey. May the blessing of
our God be with you.[9]

When you take the step of saying good-bye, eventually you'll say
good-bye to your grief and hello to a new life.

Chapter Eight

MY MOTHER DIED

The death of a parent at any time is a major loss to a child. It changes your life in so many ways and brings with it the loss of certain hopes and dreams. It can be not only the death of part of your past but part of the present and future as well. If your past with your mother was lacking, you may have been looking forward to a new future with her. But that is gone. Perhaps you had a list of questions to ask, grievances to share, or a confrontation that you had waited years to express. That opportunity is lost along with your mother.

Your identity undergoes a change, and in a way you feel orphaned. Your sense of loss is affected by your mother's spiritual condition as well—whether she was a believer or not. If your mother died at a young age, you also mourn the opportunities you feel she lost, for the years she would never live, and the dreams she would never fulfill. Her death can lead you to question what her life was for and what it meant.

> *Sometimes I feel like a motherless child . . . a long way from home.*
> —African-American spiritual

> *My mother died recently, and suddenly I wanted to go home and be a child again.*
> —Laura Scott[1]

I miss being someone's daughter. . . . So now I go through life with one less person keeping an eye on me, one less person loving me.
—Joyce Maynard[2]

When a mother dies it affects your perception of your life. When you look back at your life before your mother died, you will have a tendency to describe those times in light of her death. As one woman said, "I've divided my life into two sections: with Mom and without Mom. And I infuse the 'with Mom' memories with the knowledge she wouldn't be around at a certain point in time. What I've discovered I've done is to make the hard times we had harder, the good times better and mistakes I made were magnified."[3]

Another woman said, "I not only lost my mother when she died, I lost part of my childhood. I was eight when she left, and what I should have experienced as a child was torn away from me. I grew up missing out, like there was a hole inside of me and a hole in my future. It's like something was ripped out of me that was irreplaceable. Many of the things I should have learned about life from my mother I never learned. I guess even today I feel cheated."

UNSPEAKABLE LOSS

If you were quite young when your mother died, you were in every sense at a loss for words—even if you had a vocabulary to talk about losing Mom. The flood of feelings you had at that time and couldn't understand was so powerful it probably overwhelmed any of your thinking abilities that did exist at your young age. You didn't have any organizing framework in which to put the loss.[4]

Adults usually start working through their grief immediately after a loss. Children aren't capable of grieving as adults, so they go in and out of grief and do it in bits and pieces. At times they're angry and then sad, and then they seem to have no regard for what happened. It's difficult to stand severe emotional pain for an extended period. If you experienced the loss of your mother as a child, you probably re-grieved her loss at different times as you grew through childhood and adolescence. This could have occurred at significant developmental transitions or as you developed in your level of insight and understanding.

If your mother died when you were young, were you allowed to participate in her dying? Some families keep a mother's prognosis from a child. In 1892, Eleanor Roosevelt's mother contracted diphtheria after a surgery. Exhausted from years of trying to cope with her alcoholic husband, she did not want to live; the children were divided up "for the time being" among family members. That winter day before Christmas, as eight-year-old Eleanor stood by a window pondering the confusion in her life, an aunt, Susie Parish, walked in and told her, "Your mother is dead." That death took away Eleanor's hope of winning her mother's love. She would live with a menagerie of ifs: "If she had been more jolly, more attractive, more compatible, better behaved, would her mother have lived?"[5] These questions haunted her throughout her life.

> With her mother's death, Eleanor became an outsider, always expecting betrayal and abandonment. . . . For the rest of her life her actions were in part an answer to her mother. If she were really good, then perhaps nobody else would leave her, and people would see the love in her heart.[6]

Lost Opportunities

The early death of a mother robs a daughter of memories. As a result, she sometimes makes up her own memories, which often idealize her mother. Daughters who lose their mothers to early death are frozen in time. They had no chance to see their mother grow and change or display weaknesses and strengths. In other words, they didn't see their mother as a real person, so they may have invented in their mind the mother they wanted to have.

Author Therese Rando had this insightful comment on the death of a parent: "Like a community or institution which loses its archives in a fire, we have been stripped of a form of documentation of our lives and our history. We also have lost the direct links to our past and to unremembered parts of ourselves."[7]

When a mother dies, something else also dies—the buffer between you and death. If both of your parents have died, you are now the older generation. There's no generation in front of you to insulate you. You're much more aware of your mortality.[8]

There's another change as well. "With the death of your parent you lose opportunities also to atone or make up for unpleasantness in the past or to have further contact in the future. Along with this you may feel quite grieved over the fact that you couldn't have helped your parent in the way you would have liked. You may recall how this person always would help you out, how she constantly took care of you first before herself, how she could always fix what was wrong. Now you are in a position where you would want to return the favors to help. To take care of, to correct so she doesn't have to die. Your sadness and frustration at not being able to make it 'all better' . . . can be powerful."[9]

What have women said about the loss of their mother?

I can no longer hear her voice, as hard as I try. I would give so much to hear her say my name again.

Every time I have a new, what I call "grown-up" experience, I miss her. I want her here. I've even said, "Mom, why aren't you here? I need you! When I graduated, you weren't there, you were supposed to be. When I got married, you weren't there; you were supposed to be. When Sally was born, you weren't there; you were supposed to be. Whenever I get some exciting news, I want so much to share it with you. I can't, you're gone."

Hope Edelman suggests grief for a mother never disappears for good. She says, "When you lose a mother, the intervals between grief responses lengthen over time, but the longing never disappears. It always hovers at the edge of your awareness, prepared to surface at any time, in any place, in the least expected ways. Despite popular belief to the contrary this isn't pathological, it's normal. And it's why you find yourself at 24 or 35 or 43 unwrapping a present or walking down an aisle or crossing a busy street, doubled over and missing your mother because she died when you were seventeen."[10]

> When it comes to our relationships with our deceased mothers, many of us are locked in an emotional time warp. Regardless of how far we've come in other areas of our lives, personal or professional, our relationships with our mothers are the same now as they were at the time of our mothers' deaths.
>
> A daughter's attitude toward her mother's death, says Dr. Joyce Fraser, a psychologist in St. Claire Shores, Michigan, reflects where she is emotionally at that time in her life. Daughters who are "less involved" in their relationships with the mothers see the world through the "prism of their own needs," she adds. Often these daughters are very angry over their mothers' deaths, which they may view as abandonment. "Who is going to take care of me?" they ask themselves and the world. "Why did you leave me?" In a more evolved mother-daughter relationship, the death is viewed more as a natural part of the life cycle, even though these daughters still grieve the loss.
>
> Unless we work on issues with our mothers that remain after their deaths, we can be trapped in an emotional suspended animation.[11]

A parent's death may seem like the beginning of your own death, the first pull of yourself toward that great darkness. It strikes home with real force: "If they can die, then so can I!" You have to work through the implication of this for a long time during bereavement.[12]

Coming to Terms With a Death

If a mother dies after a long-term illness, other losses were probably experienced along the way, such as the other parent's attention and involvement, financial adjustments, and the family's way of life. Perhaps the daughter had to function as a caregiver. And how the mother handles the illness as well as facing her death influences her daughter.

If the death was from a long-term illness, much of the grieving occurs prior to the death, which allows children to give up dreams and expectations for their relationship with their parent piece by piece.

A sudden death is more difficult for many reasons. The impact is overwhelming.

* The need to blame someone else for what happened is extremely strong.
* A sudden death often involves medical and legal authorities.
* It often elicits the sense of helplessness on the part of the survivor.
* It leaves the survivor with many regrets and a sense of unfinished business.
* There is a need to understand why the death happened, not only to know the cause, but also to ascribe the blame. Sometimes God is the only available target, and it is not uncommon to hear someone say, "I hate God."
* It throws the remainder of the family into a crisis.
* It teaches children and even adults that relationships are not permanent and can end at any time and in any way. The younger the child, the more this can affect their personality development.

The Emotional Fallout

Some mothers served as the glue that held a fragile family together. Some of us grieve for a mother *and* for a family that disintegrated after death. Some siblings have been on their best behavior while their mother was dying. Nothing— including family dysfunction—was allowed to upset Mother. That fragile truce continued in some families through the rituals; in others, all it took to unravel was divvying up

Mom's estate. A punch bowl can become a battleground that resurrects old family issues. The family has never been the same—and never will be. Family histories may be divided BMD and AMD: *before* Mom's death and *after* Mom's death.[13]

A mother's death can make shambles of schedules, priorities, agendas, commitments—sometimes, our most intimate relationships. A mother's last breath inevitably changes us. Motherlessness can be paralyzing or it can be empowering. It can cause us to take life far more seriously.[14]

Sudden death is more often heard than witnessed. Because of this, you may feel anguish, wondering what your mother's last moments were like, whether they were terrifying or painful.

It is natural for their seconds or minutes of dying to become your hours of emotional distress. Turning off your thoughts by sheer willpower alone is not easy and often impossible. At some point, you may need to talk to someone.

YOU MAY NEED TO TALK TO SOMEONE

The fact that you weren't there when she died can also be a source of long-lasting regret. The fact that *no one* may have been there can also be stressful. You may have to deal with the painful mental process of second-guessing, *if only* your mother had consulted a doctor earlier and so on. Sudden deaths are often bizarre, like nightmares because they are so unexpected. This is especially true when they are accidents.[15]

To some extent, it is possible to experience survivor guilt after any death, even if the death wasn't part of some disaster. Why should we still be alive when someone else has died?

If only you had called the ambulance an hour earlier, *if only* you had persuaded Mom to give up her job last year. Surely there must have been something you could have done?

Survivor guilt deals with the fact that we still consider ourselves responsible and powerful in the face of death, even though all the evidence proves otherwise. When we're used to making life better by our own efforts, it's hard to let go and admit there was absolutely nothing we could do.

Linked to this is a certain uneasy feeling that our own need to live somehow contributed to your parent's death.

"Until Mom got sick, I was eager to get married and have a baby. We had a wedding date all lined up, but she didn't live to see the wedding. I feel kind of superstitious about my plans, as if by planning my life I was being too selfish for her. My plans, my wanting to move ahead, took too much of her energy.

"When she was finishing with life, I seemed to be just starting my own. I had a need to live, she had a need to die. Neither of us could change, but the contrast made me feel guilty."

The fact that a parent's death removes the buffering generation between ourselves and death can also mean that guilt blends into fear. Thoughts of "it might be me next" or "it could have been me" are common.

You may have to come to terms with guilt over "not being good enough" as a child. The child's self-centeredness can be profound— that feeling that you're somehow responsible for everything.[16]

With a sudden death you end up feeling helpless and powerless. There's a confusion over what happened with feelings of regret and guilt even months or years later.

It's important to return objectively (as much as possible) to the event and consider several questions. "In regard to my mother's death . . ."[17]

What was I able to do?

_____

_____

What was I unable to do?

_____

_____

What were others unable to do?

_____

_____

What made me feel that I was able to help?

_____

_____

What made me feel powerless to help?

_____

_____

Now I realize:

_____

_____

What I miss most about her now is . . .

_____

_____

SAYING GOOD-BYE

Even when a daughter carries painful memories of her relationship with her mother, death carries a sting. It signifies an end to those intense years that have taken such a toll in her life. The events themselves can never be forgotten, but the pain of the memories must be dealt with or they can keep a daughter snared by unhappiness.[18]

When a mother dies, one of the most common issues involves good-byes that were said or not said. Sometimes good-byes are verbal while others are nonverbal. How did your mother say good-bye?

If she didn't or was unable to, how might she have said it? Describe how you would have liked her to say good-bye to you and how you would have liked to say good-bye to your mother.

It is still possible for a peacemaking good-bye to occur. You can write your mother a detailed good-bye letter and read this out loud either at the gravesite or to an empty chair. Some have a gathering of friends at a "good-bye gathering" similar to a memorial service. Sometimes after a mother's death, a daughter is able to see her mother truthfully. You might lose a person but at the same time discover them anew.

What do you know about your mother?[19]

What I know about my mother's childhood:

_____

_____

What I know about my mother's adolescence:

_____

_____

When she was young she wanted to be:

_____

_____

My mother accomplished:

_____

_____

What she liked was:

_____

_____

What she loved was:

_____

_____

Those she was closest to were:

_____

_____

My mother's relationship with her mother was:

_____

_____

Mom was happiest when:

_____

_____

Mom was saddest when:

_____

_____

What upset her the most was:

_____

_____

Eight adjectives describing how my mother acted toward me:

_____

_____

What my mother was to me:

_____

_____

What I was to my mother:

_____

_____

Mom would like to be remembered for:

_____

_____

GAINING CLOSURE

When a woman has lost her mother during childhood or adolescence, her grieving is often incomplete because she didn't have the ability at the time to process the grief. And so at significant developmental times the grief will return. It could hit at a graduation; her first date; prom; her sixteenth, eighteenth, or twenty-first birthday; when she marries; when she has a child.

Although your mother isn't around to see or hear you, what I suggest you do is really for yourself, and it is not dependent upon any other person's response. Write a letter to your mother as if she were alive and could read your letter. The only difference is that you might be more explicit in the letter, knowing she isn't going to be reading it. Daughters who have had very positive relationships with their mothers have written letters, sharing how much they loved their mother, how much they miss her, and what they wish they would have said to her. Whether your relationship was positive or negative, the result can be the same for you. Once you've written this and read it aloud, you don't have to carry these thoughts around anymore in your heart and mind. Write something for each of the five categories below until there's nothing more to say.[20] Put the letter away. Sometime in the future you may want to take it out and read it again.

- What I would like to tell my mother
- What I would like her to tell me
- What I would like to ask my mother

- What I would like my mother to ask me
- What my mother would like me to know

I bring my mother back to life,
her eyes still green, still laughing.
She is still not fashionably thin.
She looks past me
for the girl
she left her old age to.
She does not recognize her
in me, a graying woman
older than she will ever be.

How strange that in the garden
of memory where she lives
nothing ever changes;
the heavy fruit
cannot pull the branches
any closer to the ground.[21]

Dear Mom,

How's the weather in heaven? Is it sunny? It's been kind of cloudy lately here. I was just thinking about you and thought I'd write. I really miss you, Mom. My life is going really well and I wish you could be a part of it. The other day I jogged by where you and Dad and I used to live. I was too young to remember that house, but I remember the playground you used to take me to. It seems a lot smaller now. I visited you at the cemetery once around Christmas, and I'm sorry I didn't go again. It's just that I don't picture you there. I picture you alive and with me every day. Please make a special effort to be with me this Monday when I take my exam on the Bible; I could use some inside information. I love you, Mom. Please look over Dad and Paul; I don't think they let you know how they feel as openly as I do. Give my love to Jupiter and Mozart. The house seemed empty without Jupiter's barking, and I

still miss Mozart's chirping. I feel better knowing they're with you.
I envy them for that. Please keep in touch and let me know when
you receive this letter—I'm not sure about the postage.
> *Love always,*
> *Sheri*[22]

Memories of your mother will fade—her fragrance, the sound of her voice, availability—but our hope is that these losses will be offset by a growing sense of peace in your heart.

Chapter Nine

HEALING THE MOTHER-DAUGHTER RELATIONSHIP

The mother-daughter relationship cuts deep and involves a vast array of experiences and emotions that sometime conflict. In this book you have read testimonies of women who have similar desires and hurts to yours. In our national survey, we asked women what they appreciate most—and least—about their mother's involvement in their lives. Here's what some wrote:

> The older I get, the more I am learning to see my mother through different eyes. I am coming to grips with the reality that you do the best you know how, and when you know better, you do better. It has been difficult, but I have accepted the fact that my mom largely had what she understood to be our best interests at heart. She acted on what she knew at the time. I think that had she realized what was at stake almost twenty years ago—the long-term ramifications of certain things—life would have been much different. Not necessarily better, but different.

> Because of my mom, I made it my top priority not to be involved with or marry a non-Christian man. I found a husband who is very loving and caring; a great father and

partner. On the other hand I've had a hard time with self-image, trust, depression, and love.

I appreciate most that she started leaving me alone, and that is when I began to grow. The least: Never feeling liked and certainly not loved!

I appreciate that her negativism and abuse taught me to overcome. Her hatred taught me to love myself and others with God's love. He has lifted the self-hatred she taught me.

I appreciate that she has always been there during hardships, but I don't appreciate her wanting us to care for her all the time when she is capable of taking care of herself. She has it in her head that because she took care of Grandma all those years, we need to take care of her.

I appreciate that even during rough times my mom stayed with our family. It is important for families to stick together. Unfortunately—and ironically—our family is very splintered now and not close at all. What I don't appreciate is how selfish my mother is. For example, for birthdays and Christmas she buys gifts that *she* wants, not what the person wants.

I appreciate how she poured her morals into me through non-threatening stories. I heard them a million times. Her spirit was one that was inviting—she was relationship smart. I didn't like that she tolerated my dad's verbal and occasional physical abuse—or his threats to kill her if she (and her paycheck) ever left him.

My mom can be very critical. I remember being so excited when she moved close to me. I was looking forward to having someone to run errands with. It only took one trip to realize that it was no fun to shop with someone who tells you what you should or shouldn't buy. At the same time, I most appreciate knowing that my mom is always there for me if I need her.

I most appreciate her love and knowledge of the Lord and her unconditional love for me all the time; the mercy and grace and encouragement she showed. She always reminded me what a great husband I had. The least: She didn't trust my godly experience and have faith that God would do great things with her marriage too. She was always afraid.

I appreciate that she *was* involved with me—that she was a part of my daily life, that she loved me, cared for me, listened to me, played with me, laughed with me, cried with me, argued with me, made up with me, respected me, and liked to be with me. I wasn't just a kid to be seen and not heard, or a nuisance to be shipped off to day care, or a bother to be tolerated until I grew up and moved away from home. I was a valued part of her life, and that fact alone had an amazingly positive influence on my life.

Her love and nurturing when I was young set me up to trust God and believe in His love for me. That was an important step in my spiritual growth. Her faithfulness to regularly attend church was also a positive influence.

I appreciate that she gave birth to me even though she didn't want me. I don't appreciate her ability to block out horrible things that happened in our family—to herself and her seven children. The unwritten law was "get married [if pregnant] or have an abortion." She would never have an abortion, but she was all for her daughters having them. Most of my sisters had abortions.

I don't appreciate that she put me in the middle of her arguments with my dad. That was horrible and painful and unfair. I still carry those emotional scars.

STARTING A NEW RELATIONSHIP

What can a daughter do to build a new relationship with her mother? Before deciding on your approach, we've got ten more questions for you, including some that build upon issues brought up earlier in the book.

1. What were your beliefs and misbeliefs about your mother as a child? Can you describe how and why these developed? How did these affect you as a child?

2. What are your current beliefs and misbeliefs about your mother? Are your current beliefs accurate? Have they been checked out with someone else or your mother? How do they affect you? In a positive or negative way— which of these would you either like to change or lessen their impact upon your life?

3. What were and are your fears about your mother? If these are current fears, what can you do to overcome them?

4. Do you have any names or labels for your mother that keep you from having a better relationship with her at this time? If you were to eliminate these names or labels, how would that affect your relationship? If these names were positive, how would this fill up your life?

5. What responses or behaviors bother you whenever you talk with your mother or see her? Have you considered giving your mother permission to say or do what she does? If you can, it diminishes the power of what she does or says. Tell yourself, "I wish she didn't say or do what she does, but I can handle this. It doesn't mean it's true and it doesn't have to affect me. I'm not perfect and neither is Mom, so what she says doesn't mean it's true.

She's probably never had any help to assist her in changing what she says and does. Mom isn't and never was perfect—that's okay."

6. Identify the areas of beliefs you have in common with your mother. These are the things you share in common. It can include religious beliefs, men, aging, health, abortion, fears, friends, foods, clothes, TV preferences, use of time, stores, spending, etc. Identify the areas in which you differ. Is this or has this been a problem? Has either of you attempted to force the other to reject what they believe and accept the other person's point of view?

7. What *don't* you know about your mother? If you had to describe your mother's life in detail and describe what happened to make her the way she is today, what would you say? Are there gaps in what you know? If so, is this because your mother didn't talk about these areas, or because you've never asked?

8. As you reflect on things your mother said to you or her rules and guidelines for your life, you probably had beliefs about why your mother said or did what she did. You have your own set of reasons. Could there be other reasons that you've never considered? One woman said:

"My mother was so cautious with me. She hovered over me and restricted my activities. It was as though I was on a leash. I grew up thinking she didn't trust me, nor did she think I was capable. When I was forty I learned that Mom had an accident riding her trike when she was three. She broke her arm and was in a coma for two weeks. I guess that trauma caused her to worry about me."[1]

9. How old is your mother? What was her culture and generation like when she was your age? What did her mother teach her about life? About parenting? It could be she lived her formative years at a time when beliefs about women, working mothers, divorce, abortion, etc., were different than what you have experienced. You and your mother will differ. You can't expect her to always agree with you, or you to always agree with her. It's all right to differ. And as she ages she will become more set in her ways just as you will. Sometimes a simple question will make the difference: "Mother, how could I make your life better for you?" You may be able to do as she asks, or maybe you won't. But you've shown that you care regardless of your past or present relationship.

10. Finally, if you decide to encourage your mother to change, what can you do? (Consider your own ideas, but also read on.)

CHANGING YOUR RELATIONSHIP

To achieve peace with your mother, what needs to change? Your mom, you, or the relationship in general? A lot depends on your attitude.

"There is no way I would ever ask my mother to change. She won't change. As much as I'd like that, it's not going to happen." This is a cry of frustrated futility coupled with longing! Beliefs keep us from making a simple request.

"Mom won't change. Our relationship won't change." This belief becomes a self-fulfilling prophecy. It cripples motivation, thwarts desire, and destroys hope.

Consider some of the beliefs that I've heard daughters give for not asking their mom to change:

- *"She isn't capable of changing."* Yes, she might be entrenched in her responses, but could it be you haven't found the right combination to unlock her resistance? The potential for change *is* there.

- *"There's nothing she could do at this point to improve our relationship."* The question to ask is: Have you identified what you want to be different? Once you know that in specific terms, you'll be able to develop a plan to talk it over.

Be sure you reinforce any change at all on the part of your mother. Thank her. It helps to focus on any positive improvement that you see. For you, it might not have been much effort to do what your mom did, but for her, it was probably a giant step. Look for the exceptions in her typical responses and behaviors. When you choose to look for these, it gives you hope that your mother is capable of changing.

- *"If I try something different, it may make matters worse. I don't want to add to the problem."* This usually means, "I have too much pain, and it hurts too much to try." But doing something different doesn't necessarily mean it will make matters worse. With new information, new understanding, and new approaches, there's a greater possibility that change can happen. If you pay attention to the smallest changes—the slightest difference on your mom's part—you could find hope again. If your next attempt at change doesn't succeed, you may be tempted to think, *I knew it wouldn't work. It isn't worth it.* Challenge the thinking. Tell yourself, "All right, it didn't work this time, but at least I tried. Let's see how I can change my response for the next approach."
- *"It's been so many years of this. She's immovable. The damage is too great."* I've seen some relationships restored that surprised even me. They did look hopeless. Look for the fears that keep you from responding. Remember, we haven't been called to live in fear. "For God did not give us a spirit of timidity, but a spirit of power, of love and of self-discipline" (2 Timothy 1:7).

It's true! Sometimes the interaction an adult daughter has with her mom is consistently less than satisfying. It's a pain. Each time there's a get-together it seems to be a continuation of creating tension and distance rather than improvement and drawing closer.

What about you? What's your interaction like at this time? There are no right or wrong answers, but completing this analysis could help you identify the rough spots, which is the first step in resolving them.[2]

1. Often I can't seem to find the right words to express what I want to say to Mom.

_____ True   _____ False

2. I'm concerned that I if share my real concerns or feelings, I'll end up being rejected by Mom and the door will be shut.

_____ True   _____ False

3. Often I don't say what I really want to because I'm not sure if my opinion is right.

_____ True   _____ False

4. If I speak up, it will only make matters worse rather than better.

_____ True   _____ False

5. I tend to do most of the talking, and Mom doesn't say much.

_____ True   _____ False

6. I don't look forward to face-to-face conversations with Mom.

_____ True   _____ False

7. I don't look forward to phone conversations with Mom.

_____ True   _____ False

8. Once we begin to argue, I keep on going and don't know how to stop.

_____ True   _____ False

9. I tend to blame her and focus on what she did or didn't do in the past.

_____ True   _____ False

10. I tend to be defensive.

_____ True   _____ False

11. I have a hard time listening to Mom.

_____ True   _____ False

12. I respond in like manner to how my mother is—anger for anger, insult for insult.

_____ True   _____ False

13. I rarely bring up significant things to talk about.

_____ True   _____ False

14. Sometimes I don't share everything, in order to cover the truth.

_____ True   _____ False

15. I think Mom needs to hear about the problem she's caused.

_____ True   _____ False

16. When I have a complaint it sounds like anger.

_____ True   _____ False

17. There are a number of issues I won't bring up with Mom.

_____ True   _____ False

18. I don't like to argue with Mom since it doesn't accomplish anything.

_____ True   _____ False

EXPECT RESISTANCE

If you make the choice to ask for change, don't be surprised if you encounter some resistance. Most everyone will resist others' efforts to get them to change. People resist change even if it's for their benefit. And there are predictable forms of resistance. Some mothers refuse to listen. They tune out. Their concern is, "If I let her know I've heard the request, I will be expected to change. I'd rather ignore her than have that pressure."

PEOPLE RESIST
CHANGE EVEN
IF IT'S FOR
THEIR BENEFIT

—☕—

Another response is to agree to change without having any intention of doing so. A mom might say, "I'll see. Sounds like a good idea," but it's only a way to placate her daughter.

Still another response is a counterattack. Mom turns the request around and begins to focus on what her daughter needs to do. Some moms especially criticize and are very good at this. One of the worst forms of resistance is to increase or intensify the very thing you're asking her to change. It can be irritating and even humiliating.

Whatever form of resistance you experience, it has one purpose: Your mom hopes you'll give up—abandon the effort. Have you experienced any of these responses in your previous attempts to bring about a change? If so, that may be why you aren't too interested in trying again for change. One of the best ways to reduce your frustration is to give your mother, at least in your heart and mind, permission to resist. It's all right. It's normal. And you can handle it. Don't let any form of resistance throw you off. Just be gently persistent.

What do you really want at this time in your life? When you think of building a new relationship with your mother, what is it you want to happen? If you want her to admit some wrongdoing or somehow make up for what you were lacking in the past, is that realistic? Is it even possible? And if she did that, how would that really change your life or fulfill you? The past cannot be changed. But you *can* do something about the present and the future. You can create present and future change. One of the ways to determine what you want to happen is by answering three sentences, stating the way things are right now.

I am . . .

_____

_____

You are . . .

_____

_____

We are . . .

_____

_____

Now ask yourself how you would like the relationship between you and your mother to be if everything were perfect.

If our relationship were perfect:

I would . . .

_____

_____

You would . . .

_____

_____

We would . . .

_____

_____

How does this compare with how your relationship looks at this time? Is it realistic, or are there huge gaps between the two? To bring a balance to your responses, complete these three sentences.

Realistically:

I could . . .

_____

_____

You could . . .

_____

_____

We could . . .

_____

_____

Now think of what you could do to make this a *reality*. Reconciliation won't just happen magically. There are several factors to consider.

How will you approach your mother if she is someone you have had difficulty with over the years?

What exactly will be your opening remarks, and then what would you like to say to your mother and what would you like your mother to say to you?

How are you feeling about approaching Mom? Are you afraid? If so, what do you think causes this fear? Perhaps there's ambivalence. You must identify these feelings, because they could cripple your efforts.[3]

REQUESTING A CHANGE

There are several steps to take when requesting a change. First of all, consider making it in writing. This gives your mother time to mull over the request for a while. It can keep her from arguing with you and may prevent a quick, negative response to the request.

WORDS THAT ARE VAGUE OR GENERAL CAN BE CONFUSING

Try to make just one request each time. If you bring up several, it can be an overload and overwhelm her.

Were you aware that there are positive intentional statements that you could make in ten seconds or less? It doesn't have to be an abundance of words. A principle you could follow is found in Proverbs 25:11 (AMP): "A word fitly spoken and in due season is like apples of gold in a setting of silver."

In today's vernacular we could say, "The right word at the right time, how good it is." And it's not only important *what* you say, but *how* you say it.

Be bottom-line and specific in what you're requesting. Words that are vague or general can be confusing. And point to the desired behavior rather than focusing on what someone hasn't done. Requests like the following don't work well:

- "You're trying to control me."
- "You don't seem to listen to me."
- "You don't show an interest in my job."
- "Why is it you never want to talk about the divorce with me?"

Your mother will probably defend herself with an isolated example of when she gave the desired response. And she feels attacked as well. Remember to point toward the desired behavior. Your mother won't feel attacked, and the request carries with it the unspoken statement: "I believe you can do it!" Here are some examples:

- "Mom, I really appreciate it when you suggest and even say, 'You can figure it out.' It makes me feel special."
- "Mom, I appreciate when you listen to me when I'm sharing something, and you let me know you've heard me. I feel understood when that happens."
- "Mom, it really helps me when you ask how I'm doing in my job. It gives us more to talk about and I feel more like an adult."
- "Mom, I have a number of questions about the divorce. I know it might be painful to talk about it, but when you're ready, I'd like to listen. This would help me understand myself better."

Notice that these statements point to the behavior you want as well as let her know how you feel, which can help her understand.

Give Her Some Time

If your mother's personality is that of an introvert, don't expect her to respond immediately to your questions. Introverts need to think before they speak, and they need silence around them to help them process their answers. They often take seven to ten seconds to answer a question, so if you don't have any immediate responses, don't assume she hasn't heard you or she's ignored you. Don't repeat your question. Give her time.

What if your mother begins to object and tries to argue? This is where you stand your ground. The way in which you do this is important. You can be calm, definite, and persistent, even if Mother is loud or irate. As we said in an earlier chapter, it helps to learn to use the "broken-record" technique. When you repeat what you have to say (whether it's an answer or a request) again and again, she will eventually begin to yield. Just come back and repeat your request with a proper tone of voice. If you are responding to an unreasonable request on her part, repeat, "No, I'm unable to do that," and eventually it works.

When you're asked for other reasons (and you will be), just repeat the same statements. You don't have to give your reasons. If you do, you will be handing Mom more power. This broken-record technique may be different for you, but it works, and it could surprise your mother.[4]

Giving Up the Dream

You may need to accept your mom the way she is. Despite your best intentions and efforts, you might find out that Mom is Mom, and she'll continue on as before.

Acceptance can mean giving up the dream of your mother changing or becoming who you would like her to be. After you have creatively and patiently taken the steps we have suggested, you may find that your mother is determined not to change. Even when people want to change, they may feel incapable of doing so. Instead of fighting it, you can choose to accept your mom's resistance or incapacity to change.

Be Creative

Part of building a better relationship with your mother is establishing better boundaries. It may take time and several attempts to build a better relationship. In many cases you may not need to bring up past issues to build a better present. You can't change past issues, and you can't extract payment. (Some issues will need addressing, however.) If you dread talking or getting together, but it's a necessity, don't do so with negative expectations; you could make them come true. Be different. Do the unexpected. Be friendly. Don't get hooked into old communication patterns. Ignore it when you're baited to repeat past issues or discussions. All families have unspoken rules of behavior and communication. Change them. Violate the rules in a healthy way. Give a different greeting. Ask different questions. Talk to others in a different way. If you're an expander (loads of detail), condense. If you're a condenser (brief, one-word responses), expand and give loads of detail. Don't ask standard questions or those that elicit a simple *yes* or *no* response. If you usually sit, stand. If you usually stand or walk around, sit. Sit in different chairs. Take a different chair at dinner. Arrange the table differently. Will it work? It may create a different atmosphere, or it may not. It's worth the effort.

Show your mother you're different. If you do something different, it can throw her, and you won't have to play old family games. The reason any game continues is that you have players. So don't play. Break the pattern. When you see your mom, do you talk in the age you are now—or are you a six-, twelve-, or sixteen-year-old in her presence?

Establish Your Purpose

Many daughters want to reconnect with their mother, but they need to consider their purpose. Is it just to make contact, to win some admission, or is it to actually gain reconciliation with her? If it's reconciliation you're after, you will need to give your mother time to process what you are sharing.

If your purpose is reconciliation, then proceed with two intentions: one, to improve the relationship, and the other, to share your perspective. Make sure it's not to punish her or walk out of her life forever. Before you meet, write out what you would like to say and read it aloud.

How has your mother responded to you in the past? With silence, criticism, blame, anger, abandonment? Why should you expect anything different now? You're the one who wants it different, and you probably have better skills to make it happen as well. You want the change. Be willing to hear her side. If your mother is reserved and quiet, there's a lot you don't know.

Both you and your mother have a point of view that is valid. Meet your mother with the attitude, "What can I learn about Mom and myself from our get-together?"

When you meet with your mother, state your purpose. Point toward what you want. Blame only activates defensiveness.

Here are some sample statements:

- "Mom, I would like our relationship to be better. I want to work toward that and wondered if you would help me in the process."
- "Mom, I would like to talk with you about us. There are some areas that trouble me, and I want to make things better."
- "Mom, I have some questions I've never asked before. It would help me to understand you and us if I could ask them."

Now you've stated your purpose. The next step may be a bit more difficult for you. It's taking responsibility for your own part in making the relationship what it was.

- "Mom, I think I expected too much from you in the past. I'm letting go of those expectations, and we can see where we go from there."
- "Mom, I know it must have been painful for you the year I didn't talk to you and didn't respond to your messages. I don't want that to happen again."
- "Mom, I said some hard things to you when I was in college. I didn't understand what was going on in your life. I'm sorry for what I said."

The next step is future oriented. Make a statement about what you would like your relationship to be in the future. This is not about placing blame or rehashing the past. It's a positive description of the changes you would like to see occur.

- "Mom, I'd like us to be able to sit down and talk about significant topics whenever I come over."
- "Mom, there's a lot I don't know about you when you were growing up. I'd have a more complete picture of who you are if you could share that with me. And I'll really listen."
- "Mom, I want us to move on and have a fresh start. We both missed connecting with each other, and I think we can now."
- "Mom, I'm so glad the drinking and drug years are over for both

of us. We're both different now, and it's going to be better. I really like it when you call to see how I'm doing and I will do the same with you."[5]

Peace is possible. Here is how some daughters found it:

Sometimes I think I have lived my whole life trying to be all the things my mother wasn't. Before she died I came to the place of forgiveness and tried to understand the things that shaped her. I wrote her a long letter. Four days before she died she communicated for the first time how much she loved me and what a good daughter I had been.

Many years of counseling have helped me recognize and overcome what and why I have done the things I do. Also, accepting the Lord as my Savior and learning who He is and His will for me has brought me great comfort and peace.

Years ago when I was a young Christian I remember screaming into a pillow and saying I hated my mother. Then I felt the Lord tell me to get a picture of her as a young child and pray for that child. When I finished praying, one of the first things I did was forgive.

I asked Jesus how to make our relationship better. He told me to honor and love her. I call almost every day and help her as often as I can, even though we are many miles apart. I always tell her I love her.

I have come to accept my mom for who she is. I have accepted the fact that she, like myself, made many mistakes. I have learned to put "stuff" behind us and just be there for her.

I have chosen to accept my mother as she is and not try to change her. I have found humor to help in our communication and a forgiving heart in our relationship.[6]

Chapter Ten

HAVING COURAGE TO
EXPRESS YOURSELF

One of the regrets in most of life's relationships can be summed up in this phrase: "I wish I had told her . . ." Too often when others touch our lives in significant ways, we either seem to be at a loss for words that express the depth of our thoughts and feelings to that person, or we just never get around to it. There are some things that we perhaps would like to say but believe it best not to. There may be questions we have held in for years, but perhaps we're afraid of the answer we'd receive—if we got one at all.

If you could say anything to your mom, what would you like to say?

This is is one of the steps to making peace with your mother. Many daughters carry on conversations with their mothers in their mind. They rehearse what they want to say again and again. And for many, this inner conversation continues. Talking to yourself doesn't resolve much but only reinforces the agony.

The answer is expressing what you have to say to your mother. It may be directly face-to-face or in a note or letter. If she isn't available, you could still write a letter and then simply read it aloud to yourself, or if she's deceased, do it at the gravesite. The value of expressing your thoughts and feelings is just that—expressing them. It isn't dependent upon Mother's response. It doesn't matter if she responds favorably or unfavorably, thankfully or ungratefully, positively or negatively. If the value is dependent upon her response, you're allowing her to control you. It's enough just to say what's inside you. Take time to reflect on what you have to say.

In our survey we asked daughters the question, "At this point in your life, what would you like to be able to say to your mother?" The following responses may help you in your journey.

Why didn't she ever tell me she loved me? I know she did but never said it.

"What's heaven like?" And have her know the answer.

Mom, forgive me for judging you, for resenting you, for being so critical of you and your decisions. I thank God for giving you to me. I know He handpicked you for me. As God has forgiven me, I know I have to forgive you. I love you.

Even though our life was crazy, as a child you didn't really know what to do. You were as traumatized as I was, probably more, but we both survived. I love you and forgive you.

Mother, you did the best you could with what you knew. Thanks.

Thank you for never turning your back on me even when I turned from you. Thank you for your love and support.

You don't want to know. I'd curse at her, shake her, yell at her for being so *dense* and for not believing me or protecting me from her older children (children who were themselves pedophiles) and her husband (a pedophile). "Why didn't you stop having kids after the third one like you wanted to?"

Mom, I love you. I am so desperately wanting you to change everything from since you were with me. I would like you to hold me. I wanted you to tell me you loved me. I wanted you to know me as a person. I wanted you to love me as your daughter. I wanted you to know that I have feelings. I hurt, I have joy. I have sorrow and pain. I am alive. Please let us be happy together. Let us relish in your love for me. Tell me something that is in your heart. Tell me something that you love about our relationship. Tell me that I am a precious child of God and that I am loved. I am treasured. Tell me that I am a good enough person for my husband to love. Tell me that I am a person who could love and is good enough to receive it. Tell me how much sorrow you have for not being my mom. Tell me how much you wanted to love me and throw your arms around me, kiss me, and make me feel special. Don't criticize me, just love me, Mom. Love me.

I'm so sorry you have had to live with this curse of hate and negativism; you don't have to live that way. You can find true joy in God! I forgive you and I will continue to do so. There is still a chance for healing and forgiveness--God will never give up on you.

I would say, why are you so selfish? Why don't you ever call me to ask me how I'm doing? What has been so painful in your life that you live in a constant state of denial? Will you ever own up to your mistakes?

Thanks, Mom. You were God's planned mother for me and you did a wonderful job. I'm glad you adopted me. I was adopted twice—by you and Dad and by God.

Mom, I appreciate you so much. I admire you for your intelligence, common sense, and enthusiasm for life. You are a loving, thoughtful, and generous mother and grandmother.

"I miss you." I cry at this very thought—to be able to have a conversation with her. When I'm lucky I dream about her.

The dreams are vivid and real! I know she's dead, but somehow here to connect with me. I'd tell her all about my new godly husband and my kids. I'd ask her advice about my rebellious son. I'd thank her and hold her hand like we used to do. I'd drive her around town, show her all the changes. I'd tell her about my new friends and update her on the old ones. I'd call my brother so we could hang out together. I'd share a cup of coffee, she drank hers black. I'd tell her about my love affair with Jesus and how I got the strength (from Him) to leave my ex after he tried to kill me. I'd pray with her, I'd hug her and kiss her and press my cheek against hers. I'd thank her for being so incredible and tell her all the same stories she told me—which I now tell my kids. I'd treasure every single moment—her life and memory will live forever.

Mom, I really wish that I understood you. I wish I knew why you keep me at arm's length, why it was always so tough for you to express your love to me. I don't know that I remember you telling me that you loved me much. I always felt like there was something that I had to continually live up to, that I wasn't doing something right, that your expectations of me were almost more than I could handle. As a driven, oldest child, this was tough on me. Dad always wrote notes of encouragement or acted affectionate to me. Why couldn't you do this? It makes me angry and jealous when I see my friends and their relationships as adults with their mothers. It's not that I can't stand being around you— we shop after Thanksgiving and you listen to stories of your grandchild and we talk on the phone once a week, but why is there this huge void between what we say and what we actually feel?

I have chosen not to dwell on her inadequacy. It would not benefit her or me—it would only hurt. I would honestly like to tell her how I feel, but I cannot; it would kill her.

I've never felt like my mom has enjoyed being with me. When my parents used to visit, it was all about seeing the grandkids. I would love my mom to just call up one day and say, "Why don't we take a day and just hang out and get to know one another better?" I look forward to the day when she knows Christ personally and we can truly grow closer together through a common bond of the Lord, Jesus Christ.

Well done, good and faithful servant. You finished the race and you taught me to run this race with godly character and dignity and grace.

Thank you for being such a wonderful role model. You and Daddy were the greatest blessing a girl could have ever had. I will always love you and look forward to telling you this in heaven.

I'd like to say to her, "I wish you would listen to me more and value what I had to say. I wish you would call more and wouldn't be so angry and bitter over life. I wish your attitude was more positive, like it used to be when I was growing up. I wish you weren't so selfish and concerned that life has to be your way. Please don't carry grudges toward those you are angry with. But I still love you, no matter what."

I would like to be able to have an honest, open conversation about the things that hurt me. I would like to have her not interrupt me but stay silent, listen, and truly grasp perspective on these events. I would like to hear her side of the story . . . as an adult, I'm sure I'd be able to better understand where she was coming from. Was she afraid of failing? Is that why she parented with fear and guilt tactics, with legalism? Did she feel like she couldn't earn my respect and obedience so she had to extract it from me by force? It would be so healing to hear her be vulnerable with me by vocalizing some fears or doubts that she may have had.

You taught me life's most important lesson: Live a life committed to God through a daily walk with Him. Your mistakes were part of being human, and I know it was not your intention to exclude me. Even those "mistakes" have helped me grow in God's grace. I look forward to seeing you again.

Mom, thank you for being such an inspiration to me. Thank you for helping me to learn about Christ and for just being there for me in good times and in bad. Your steadfast love, concern, and prayers for me have carried me through some difficult times. Thank you for who you are and for the example you have been. I love you!

Mother, I do love you, and I wish I had not been so self-centered during those growing-up years, that I had risked opening up to you in a way that no doubt would have touched a deep well in your own heart. Please forgive me, Mother, and I pray that I will provide that opening to my own daughters and their children.

She already knows the words to my song, but mostly I just want to say, "Thank you so much, Mom. You are my best girl friend and I want to be more like you every day. I am so grateful to God for picking me to be the lucky girl who got to be your daughter."

I think I would like to say thank-you for what she has taught me and all that we have struggled through, because in it all, I have learned some very powerful, life-changing lessons. These lessons have been hard won, but also I trust they will be with me for the rest of my life, because they are hard won—and I am going to hang on, by God's grace, to these lessons. I appreciate that no matter how difficult I have been at times, and how very hard I have been on her, she has let me be who I am, and she has never let me go. We have worked and struggled at things because we both want better than we have had or known, and this means so very much to me. I would like her to know that I am working and will continue to work at shifting or changing my expectations of both her and me. Without sounding pious or self-righteous, my greatest prayer for her is that she will come to know Jesus in a personal way, and that she will be able to experience the life-changing forgiveness, grace, and hope that He longs to give her. I so badly want her to be at peace with herself and with God. I would also tell her that without her, I would not be who I am, and that if I ever have the opportunity to be a wife and mother, I will work at it with all that I am, largely because of her. I pray that that will be my best work yet. I would need her to know that I really, truly, from the bottom of all that I am, forgive her for all that has happened. That I look forward to the second half of our relationship. That I believe God has some really great things in store for both of us, and I want her along for every bit of it. My mom needs to know that I love her, I have always loved her, and that I still need her, just like I always will. I really enjoy the times that we spend together, and I look forward to some of the things that she has yet to teach me. I love to hear her laugh, and it is good to see all the love that she has to give. I am the most at peace with my mom that I ever have been, not because of who I am, but because of all that my God is.

What I would like to say is, "Mom, I want to love you and respect you. You have many good qualities, but you won't let anyone see who you really are. I want to know you. You don't have to be perfect to be loved. I want you to take better care of yourself. I want your home to be clean and safe—for you and for Dad. I want you to really love my dad and appreciate all that he's done for you for almost fifty years. I want you to tell us when you're hurting or afraid or confused or angry. It's okay to feel what you truly feel. It's not too late for us to have an honest, loving relationship."

One survey respondent for this book seemed to recognize the generational legacy that mothers can set for their daughters. She wrote, "I struggled to understand how certain areas in my relationship with my mom could be so good and other areas be bad. Growing up I saw my mom's pain from her childhood for the way she was treated by my grandmother. I'm sure my mom heard a story or two from my grandmother about hurtful times she had with my great-grandmother and so on and so on . . ."

To help in the healing process, the woman wrote the following, which she shared with us.

You Are Loved

It's weird how sometimes you love someone so much and everyone can tell, and sometimes you love someone so much and nobody can tell . . . not even the one you love.

My mother always thought that her mother didn't love her because she never told her so. I guess my mother had a hard time expressing how she felt. Maybe my great-grandmother did too.

I am able to imagine that if a conversation were to take place today between my mother and my grandmother, they would talk openly. I imagine they would express how they felt without holding any emotions back like so many people do.

I can imagine my grandmother reaching for my mother's hands and with tears in her eyes saying, "I love you. I loved all my children equally." A tear rolls down my mother's cheek as she says, "I wanted more." My grandmother squeezes my mother's hands, so as to let her know how much she cares and to not be afraid of showing her tears.

Squeezing even tighter, my grandmother would say, "What more could I have done? I took care of you the best that I knew how. I worked hard to help support you and the rest of the family. I thought I gave you everything that you needed. I'm sorry if I was not there for you."

Now my mother is crying harder and, like a child, she is longing to be held by her mother. She says almost in a whisper, "I wanted more." My grandmother, looking straight into my mother's eyes, says, "I am listening; tell me what more I could have done." My mother, with exasperation in her voice says, "I wanted to hear it. I wanted to hear you say the words, 'I love you.' I wanted a hug and a kiss with an 'I love you' every morning before going to school, and I wanted the last thing I heard at night to be you telling me that you loved me."

I picture my grandmother, with a little smile on her face, telling my mother that, as a child, she dreamed about having a little baby to love. A baby she could sing a lullaby to and rock to sleep at night. She says, "When I was pregnant I couldn't wait to hold you. The second you were born, all of my dreams came true. I looked straight at your tiny face and into those beautiful eyes of yours, vowing to always be here to wipe the tears away and to hold your hand when you were not feeling well."

I can still imagine my grandmother going on to say, "Things were harder than I expected, but I never stopped loving you. I'm sorry I couldn't show it more." With confidence in her voice she says, "You are my precious baby girl," and in an embrace, my grandmother tells my mother that she loves her. She loves her very much.

My wonderful mother has always been desperate for us to know how much she cares. When we were growing up she told us every day, many times a day, that she loved us. Even today at the end of a telephone conversation, if my mother thinks that she didn't say "I love you," she will call right back and say it. She says, "I didn't want to hang up without saying 'I love you.'" I am very grateful for this because I always know how very much I am loved.

I hope that my children will grow up feeling my love for them as much as I feel my mother's love for me.

POSTSCRIPT

As we see it, picking up this book has been an act of courage on your part. Whether it's because of issues with your mom, or mom problems faced by someone you care about, you are looking for answers, and that can be a potentially frightening and painful process.

We have looked at the impact that your mother had—and continues to have—in your life. We have seen how this mother-daughter relationship can shape how you relate to others, including your heavenly Father.

If you feel that there is still much that you need to process and work through, don't hesitate to seek out a godly counselor who can help you take the important steps necessary to make healing a reality in your life. As we have written before, there is no shame in taking advantage of all the resources that God has provided for us. He wants to see you healed, restored, and getting on with the joy of living. He is the perfect Parent who will never fail you.

By now, we hope you know that you are not alone in wanting to make peace with your mom. You have read about hurts and experiences that are probably similar to yours. You have also had some examples of positive relationships between daughters and their moms and some incidences of genuine reconciliation and peace that came out of difficult situations. To that end, we want to leave you with one last example of the blessings to be found in a mended relationship. It's expressed in a letter from Sheryl to her mom, Joyce Wright.

Dear Mom,

When Daddy asked me to be a part of this book project, I was elated. So much has changed in the past few years that this book is an opportunity to let you know how much I appreciate you.

When Shaelyn was born, I couldn't wait for you to see her. I was also sad because I knew you would have to return to Long Beach. I had waited years to become a mother so I could share the experience with you.

When you both decided to move to Bakersfield to be closer, I couldn't believe it. I never thought you would move in a million years! Now we could really share the "mothering" experience together.

You taught me the softer side of being a mother. I remember when I was about ten or eleven years old, thinking, I never want to forget how this feels so I can remember it when I have a child of my own. Fortunately, I have a lot of memories as far back as three, four, and five years old. You validated my feelings when I was very young. It was all right to be mad or angry, but how I expressed it may not be. That is one of the most important lessons you taught me that I can share with Shaelyn. This has come in handy with her. I can tell if she is mad-angry, frustrated-angry, sad-angry, or even scared-angry. One of the things she is also learning is the difference between the various types of anger.

Shaelyn and I talk about her feelings often and I tell her stories of when I was her age. I know we are all finding out how much alike Shaelyn and I are. I know how much this is a surprise to me, so I can only imagine how much it is for you.

Having parents that are so different from each other can be positive. As you know, Bill and I are different in some aspects and alike in others. I believe that we can make this a positive for Shaelyn by looking back at you and Dad's example when I was growing up.

I thank you for the opportunity to spend so much time with you, and Shaelyn appreciates spending time with you as well. You remind me in so many ways of how much the Lord is there just waiting for me to ask for help.

I tend to give things over to the Lord but also take them back after a while. You have such a kind and soft way about you when you remind me He is there for me.

When you were diagnosed with a brain tumor, I was very angry with God! I haven't told anyone this. How could He allow the move from Long Beach to Bakersfield to go so smoothly and then allow the possibility of my losing you? The grace with which you took the news, and then learning the surgeon could not remove the tumor, is what helped the anger fade into trusting that the Lord had plans for you and our family.

You took chemo and radiation with such a trust in the Lord. We can only thank the Lord and the hundreds of people who persistently prayed for you. And after you went through all the treatments, I couldn't believe that shingles would be the next physical pain you'd have to deal with! I saw you in more pain than I have ever seen in my life. Again the anger at the Lord crept back for me. How could He allow such intense pain to happen to a woman who has done nothing but trust, obey, and want to please our Lord Jesus with her entire heart?! Again, your strength made my anger turn into asking for help to become your helper for a change.

I am so thankful every day that you are here and that it wasn't your time yet to go home to the Lord. I know I am being selfish, but I need you on a daily basis. Whether it's a phone call or a hug, I can't wait to talk to you every day. Thanks for being such an amazing role model and being open about your faults as well. As outgoing as I am, I don't think you realize how much you have been responsible for that. Yes, I got a lot from Daddy, but how to share and help other people I truly learned from you. I look forward to however much time on earth we have together, knowing you and our entire family will be rejoicing and praising the Lord in heaven.

Thank you again, and please never change. You are truly a blend of many of the women described in the Bible who have made an impact not only on me, but on countless numbers of women who have had the joy of spending time with you.

I love you,
Sheryl

ENDNOTES

Chapter One
1. Henry Cloud and John Townsend, *The Mom Factor* (Grand Rapids, MI: Zondervan, 1996), 13.
2. Cloud and Townsend, 16.
3. Victoria Secunda, *When You and Your Mother Can't Be Friends* (New York: A Delta Book, Dell Publishing, 1990), xvi-xvii.
4. Nancy Wasserman Cocola and Arlene Modica-Matthews, *How to Manage Your Mother* (New York: Simon & Schuster, 1992), 13.
5. Dr. Susan Forward, *Toxic Parents* (New York: Bantam Books, 1989), 74.

Chapter Two
1. Laura Davis, *I Thought We'd Never Speak Again* (New York: Quill, 2002), 7.
2. Davis, 7.
3. Dr. Dan B. Allender, *The Wounded Heart* (Colorado Springs, CO: NavPress, 1995), 30.
4. Alyce Faye Cleese and Brian Bates, *How to Manage Your Mother* (New York: HarperCollins, 2000), 8–9.
5. Allender, 36.
6. Jane Myers Drew, PhD, *Where Were You When I Needed You, Dad?* (Newport Beach, CA: Tiger Lily Publishing, 2003), 16.

7. Some material in this chapter adapted from H. Norman Wright, *A Dad-Shaped Hole in My Heart,* (Minneapolis: Bethany House, 2005).

Chapter Three

1. Dr. Susan Forward, *Toxic Parents* (New York: Bantam Books, 1989), 59.
2. Forward, 49.
3. Nancy Wasserman Cocola and Arlene Modica-Matthews, *How to Manage Your Mother* (New York: Simon & Schuster, 1992), 74.
4. Judith Balswick, *Mothers and Daughters Making Peace* (Ann Arbor, MI: Servant Publications, 1993), 4.
5. Barbara Zax, PhD and Stephan Poulter, PhD, *Mending the Broken Bough* (New York: Berkley Books, 1998), 35.
6. Zax and Poulter, 37.
7. Deborah Tannen, *You're Wearing That?* (New York: Random House, 2006), 30–31.
8. Shanna Smith, MSW, *Making Peace With Your Adult Children* (New York: Harper Perennial, 1991), 96–110.
9. Zax and Poulter, 164–167.
10. Zax and Poulter, 191–193.

Chapter Four

1. Deborah Tannen, *You're Wearing That?* (New York: Random House, 2006), 47.
2. Judith Balswick, *Mothers and Daughters Making Peace* (Ann Arbor, MI: Servant Publications, 1993), 93.
3. Nancy Wasserman Cocola and Arlene Modica-Matthews, *How to Manage Your Mother* (New York: Simon & Schuster, 1992), 42–47.
4. Cocola and Modica-Matthews, 63.
5. Barbara Zax, PhD and Stephan Poulter, PhD, *Mending the Broken Bough* (New York: Berkley Books, 1998), 73–95.
6. Dr. Susan Forward, *Toxic Parents* (New York: Bantam Books, 1989), 61.
7. Alyce Faye Cleese and Brian Bates, *How to Manage Your Mother* (New York: HarperCollins, 2000), 82–88.

8. Cleese and Bates, 90.
9. Victoria Secunda, *When You and Your Mother Can't Be Friends* (New York: Delacorte, 1990), 107.
10. Gerald W. Piaget, PhD, *Control Freaks* (New York: Doubleday, 1991), 102–116.
11. Piaget, 147.
12. Manuel J. Smith, PhD, *When I Say No I Feel Guilty* (New York: Bantam Books, 1975), 108–109.
13. Paula Caplan, PhD, *The New Don't Blame Mother* (New York: Routledge, 2000), 1.
14. Caplan, 3.
15. Cleese and Bates, 235.

Chapter Five

1. Victoria Secunda, *When You and Your Mother Can't Be Friends* (New York: Delacorte, 1990), 5.
2. Ronald T. Potter-Efron and Patricia S. Potter-Efron, *Anger, Alcoholism and Addiction: Treating Anger in a Chemical Dependency Setting* (New York: Norton, 1991), 51–54.
3. Secunda, 159–160.
4. Paula J. Caplan, *Don't Blame Mother: Mending the Mother-Daughter Relationship* (New York: Harper & Row, 1989), 25.
5. Caplan, 22–30.
6. Caplan, 31.
7. Kathy Olson, *Silent Pain* (Colorado Springs, CO: NavPress, 1992), 11–13.
8. Some material in this chapter adapted from Gary Oliver and H. Norman Wright, *A Woman's Forbidden Emotions* (Ventura, CA: Regal Books, 2005).

Chapter Six

1. Harriet Lerner, *Women in Therapy* (Northvale, NJ: Jason Aronson, 1988), 67–87.
2. Some helpful reading would be chapter 4 of *The Dance of Anger* by Harriet Lerner; *When I Say No I Feel Guilty* by Manuel Smith;

and *When You and Your Mother Can't Be Friends* by Victoria Secunda.

3. See H.C. Leupold, *Exposition of Ecclesiastes* (Grand Rapids, MI: Baker Books, 1978), 14–155; and Franz Delitzsch, *Commentary on the Song of Songs and Ecclesiastes* (Grand Rapids, MI: Eerdmans Publishing, 1970), 318–319.

4. Dr. Charney Herst with Lynette Padwa, *For Mothers of Difficult Daughters* (New York: Villard, 1998), 159.

5. Dr. Sidney B. Simon and Suzanne Simon, *Forgiveness* (New York: Warner Books, 1991), 43.

6. Simon and Simon, 46.

7. Lewis Smedes, *The Art of Forgiving* (Nashville: Moorings, 1996), 176.

8. H. Norman Wright, *Always Daddy's Girl* (Ventura, CA: Regal Books, 1989), 234–237.

9. Smedes, 27.

10. Wright, 240–241.

Chapter Seven

1. Hope Edelman, *Motherless Daughters* (New York: Delta, 1994), xxiv-xxv.

2. Henry Cloud and John Townsend, *The Mom Factor* (Grand Rapids, MI: Zondervan, 1996), 28–29.

3. Edelman, 82–83.

4. Edelman, 176.

5. Edelman, 80.

6. *Newsweek,* July 15, 1996, 48–54.

7. Dr. David Stoop, PhD, *Making Peace With Your Father* (Ventura, CA: Regal Books, 2004), 187–211.

8. Stoop, 187-211.

9. Joyce Rupp, *Praying Our Goodbyes* (New York: Ivey Books, 1988), 20–21.

Chapter Eight

1. Laura Scott, "So Much Changes When Elders Pass Away," *The Kansas City Star,* 9 June 1995, C5.

2. Joyce Maynard, "Liberating Loss Lets Happiness Be Personal,"

The Gregonian, 13 October 1990, CL.

3. Diane Hambrook and Gail Eisenberg, *A Mother Loss Workbook* (New York: Harper Perennial, 1997), 26.

4. Maxine Harris, *The Loss That Is Forever* (New York: A Plume Book, 1995), 4.

5. Blanche Wiesen Cook, *Eleanor Roosevelt: Volume 1, 1884–1933* (New York: Viking, 1993), 79.

6. Cook, 79.

7. Therese Rando, *Grieving: How to Go On Living When Someone You Love Dies* (Lexington, MA: Lexington Books, 1988), 144.

8. Rando, 142–146.

9. Rando, 146.

10. Hope Edelman, *Motherless Daughters* (New York: Delta, 1994), 24–25.

11. Patricia Commins, *Remembering Mother, Finding Myself* (Deerfield Beach, FL: Health Communications, Inc., 1999), 54–55.

12. Fiona Marshall, *Losing a Parent* (Cambridge Center, MA: Fisher Books, 1993), 5.

13. Harold Ivan Smith, *Grieving the Loss of a Mother* (Minneapolis: Augsburg Books, 2003), 4.

14. Smith, 1.

15. Marshall, 45.

16. Marshall, 66–67.

17. Hambrook and Eisenberg, 97–98.

18. Judith Balswick, *Mothers and Daughters Making Peace* (Ann Arbor, MI: Servant Publications, 1993), 213.

19. Hambrook and Eisenberg, 33–35.

20. Hambrook and Eisenberg, 269–270.

21. "The Garden," from *Alive Together* by Lisel Mueller, published by Lousiana State University Press.

22. Edelman, 92.

Chapter Nine

1. Paula Caplan, PhD, *The New Don't Blame Mother* (New York: Routledge, 2000), 163–168.

2. Phillip C. McGraw, PhD, *Relationship Rescue* (New York: Hyperion, 2000), 41–42.

3. Dr. Sidney B. Simon and Suzanne Simon, *Forgiveness* (New York: Warner Books, 1991), 202–203.

4. Dr. Patricia Love, *The Emotional Incest Syndrome* (New York: Bantam Books, 1990), 172.

5. Love, 178–180.

6. Some material in this chapter adapted from H. Norman Wright, *A Dad-Shaped Hole in My Heart* (Minneapolis: Bethany House, 2005).

ALSO FROM H. NORMAN WRIGHT

Healing for the Dad-Shaped Hole in Her Heart

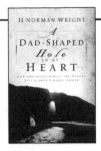

Every daughter knows how important "Daddy" is. And if he disappoints her or isn't available, she can be profoundly affected for the rest of her life. Whether abused, neglected, or abandoned, the result is an emptiness that cries to be filled. Here she can find the help she needs to face her hurt and find healing. Using Scripture, honest testimonies, and insights shared from Wright's many years of counseling experience, this book can take women from pain and heartache to renewed joy as they realize their heavenly Father has always been there for them.

A Dad-Shaped Hole in My Heart by H. Norman Wright

1 South
Circle
Super 8 Room 255